# ROYAL WALES

# Royal Wales

Deborah Fisher

UNIVERSITY OF WALES PRESS
CARDIFF
2010

*British Library Cataloguing-in-Publication Data*
A catalogue record for this book is available from the British Library.

ISBN 978-0-7083-2214-7
e-ISBN 978-0-7083-2312-0

Printed by Gutenberg Press, Tarxien, Malta

This book is dedicated to the memory of my dear uncle,
Ray Woodward (1923–2010)

# Contents

# Prologue

In 2007, a plaque was presented to the Snowdonia Society for placement in the new visitor centre at the summit of Snowdon, the highest mountain in Wales. In the Welsh language, Snowdon is called Yr Wyddfa (meaning 'the tumulus') and Snowdonia is Eryri, the 'lair of eagles'. The medieval princes of Gwynedd called themselves lords of Snowdonia, and even today Baron Snowdon is a lesser royal title (currently held by Prince Philip).

The newly carved plaque was donated by the Princess Gwenllian Society, a flourishing group that aims to preserve the memory of Princess Gwenllian (1282–1337), daughter of Llywelyn ap Gruffydd. The dispossessed princess spent most of her life cloistered in a convent in Lincolnshire, courtesy of Edward Longshanks. The Snowdonia National Parks Authority had reservations about the placing of the plaque, however. Perhaps, with its 'official' status, the authority did not wish to be associated with anything that smacked of nationalism.

Princess Gwenllian is regarded by many as the last member of the last 'true' royal family of Wales, and as such may be seen a figurehead for believers in independence. Yet, even if we temporarily disregard Owain Glyndŵr (who has a society of his own to look after his interests), we will find that Gwenllian was hardly the last of her line. The royal blood she inherited from both parents, a rich mixture of English and Welsh, is to be found in others who survived. Her uncle Rhodri has many surviving direct descendants, as have her great-aunts Gwladus and Elen. That same blood has run through the veins of every British monarch since Wales became part of 'Great' Britain and, later, the United Kingdom.

# Family Trees

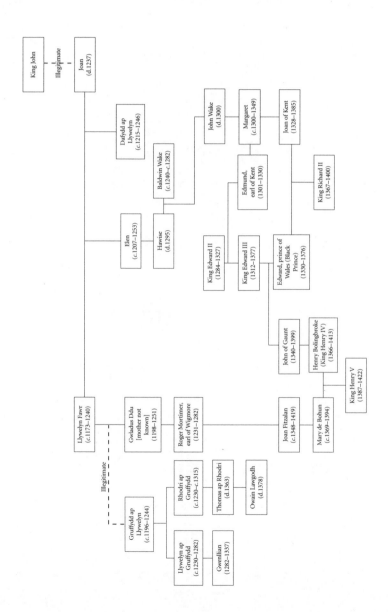

King John — Illegitimate — Joan (d.1237)

Joan (d.1237)

Llywelyn Fawr (c.1173–1240)

Dafydd ap Llywelyn (c.1215–1246)

Elen (c.1207–1253)

Hawise (d.1295)

Baldwin Wake (c.1240–c.1282)

John Wake (d.1300)

Margaret (c.1300–1349)

Edmund, earl of Kent (1301–1330)

Joan of Kent (1328–1385)

King Edward II (1284–1327)

King Edward III (1312–1377)

King Richard II (1367–1400)

Edward, prince of Wales (Black Prince) (1330–1376)

John of Gaunt (1340–1399)

Henry Bolingbroke (King Henry IV) (1366–1413)

King Henry V (1387–1422)

Gwladus Ddu [mother not known] (1198–1251)

Roger Mortimer, earl of Wigmore (1231–1282)

Joan Fitzalan (c.1348–1419)

Mary de Bohun (c.1369–1394)

Gruffydd ap Llywelyn (c.1196–1244) — Illegitimate

Rhodri ap Gruffydd (c.1230–c.1315)

Llywelyn ap Gruffydd (c.1230–1282)

Thomas ap Rhodri (d.1363)

Owain Lawgodh (d.1378)

Gwenllian (1282–1337)

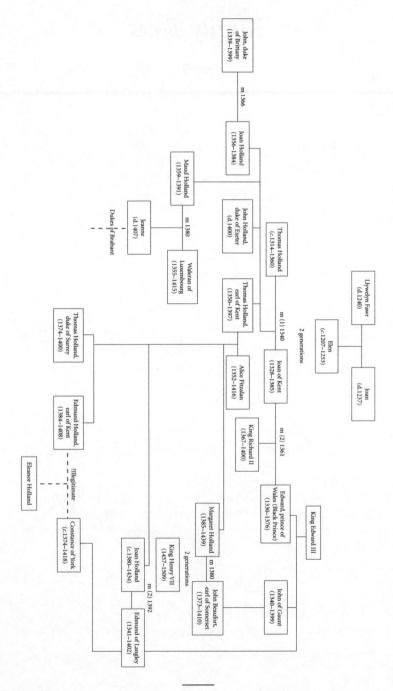

# Illustrations

# Introduction

When King Edward I brought about the death of the last independent prince of Wales, he was eliminating a royal family with which he had close blood ties. Llywelyn's late wife, Eleanor de Montfort (1252–82), had been Edward's first cousin. Llywelyn's uncle and predecessor, Dafydd, had been another first cousin. Llywelyn's aunt, Gwladus Ddu, had been married to Ralph Mortimer, lord of Wigmore, a Norman whose forebears had served Edward's ancestor, William the Conqueror, and had done well out of the invasion of England. The Mortimers had also intermarried with the English royal family, and several of their descendants would have a pivotal role to play in the future of Anglo-Welsh relations.

It was not unusual, in the Middle Ages, for close family ties to be ignored when political issues came to the fore. Just as families today may fall out over things like wills, divorce and the custody of children, so royal families in the past have squabbled and have even resorted to systematic elimination of their nearest and dearest in order to reinforce their own position. The Welsh were not above the same practice. After the death of Owain Gwynedd in 1170, his sons famously fought one another for dominance, the overall winners being 'Cristin's brood', the children of Owain's charismatic second wife. This being the case, we should hardly be surprised at the suffering English kings were prepared to inflict on their rival rulers across the border.

Throughout the Middle Ages and afterwards, not only in England and Wales but worldwide, marriages between the members of royal and noble families were made for political reasons. The idea was that the children of such marriages would inherit the parents' titles and property and that their kingdoms, principalities, fiefdoms or other types of territory would thereafter become firm allies. It seldom worked that way in practice. In Wales, rulers of small individual kingdoms were handicapped by the tradition of dividing their inheritance equally between all male children (including the illegitimate ones). Occasionally, they got around this by marrying off their sons to the daughters of other rulers, thus enabling kingdoms of a comparable size to be created. This was how men like Rhodri Mawr (*c.*820–78) and Hywel Dda (*c.*880–950) succeeded in becoming 'kings' of most of what we now call Wales.

Royalty, for many people today, is a dirty word. Republicans see it as a symbol of oppression, a legacy of the times when physical power and inherited privilege decided who held sway, times when the greatest happiness of the greatest number was not even a peripheral consideration. For others, even in Wales, the word 'royalty' embodies all that is great about the island of Britain. It symbolizes tradition, permanence and pageantry. This is not a new phenomenon; the royal families of the now United Kingdom, like those of other monarchies, have always had an ambivalent relationship with their subjects. This book examines where Wales fits into that picture.

The customs, traditions and government of the principality are in many ways inseparable from those of the UK as a whole, yet their origins in the activities of our royal families are often ignored. It is no accident that we have a prince of Wales, a Royal Welsh regiment and a Royal Welsh Show, that our towns and organizations are proud of their royal charters, that royal wedding rings are made from Welsh gold.

Unlike my two previous books published by University of Wales Press, *Princesses of Wales* and *Princes of Wales*, this book does not attempt to tell the stories of people's lives. Its goal is to explore the meaning of the word 'royal' in the context of Welsh life, uncovering unexpected connections and revealing how, even in the present day, the British royal family is indissolubly linked with its Welsh subjects. Our past has been heavily influenced by the royals; could it be that their future depends on us?

# Kings of Wales

W e cannot go back far enough in written history to find out much about the pre-Roman rulers of Wales. The earliest Welsh leader whose name we know is the man called Caradog by the Welsh and Caratacus by the Romans, and he did not originate from the region we now call Wales. A son of King Cunobelinos of the Catuvellauni, who ruled the area around Colchester, Caratacus fled westward before the Roman invaders, after the defeat of his own people, and joined forces with the Silures, the tribe native to south-east Wales. After a further defeat, he retreated north to ally himself with the Ordovices. The Iron Age earthwork at Llanymynech, known as Caer Caradoc, is traditionally believed to have been his stronghold, and there is no reason this should not be true.

With their new leader, the western tribes struggled to resist the might of the Roman army, but in AD 51 Caratacus was captured and taken to Rome. The Roman historian Tacitus, in book 12 of his *Annals*, records how the Emperor Claudius, impressed with the dignified manner of the Celtic leader, spared his life. In referring to the procession of captives and battle spoils, Tacitus uses the Latin adjective equivalent to 'regal', implying recognition of Caratacus as a king. Nevertheless, Cassius Dio, a later Roman writer, in his *Epitome*, puts these words into the mouth of the British leader as he is shown around the city of Rome: 'How can you, who have such possessions and so many of them, covet our poor tents?' Either Caratacus was playing down his own standard of living, or Tacitus was exaggerating his status so as to enhance the Roman achievement in defeating the Celts.

Whatever the truth, Caradog is a name which, from the earliest days of recorded history, has been associated with certain qualities: not merely courage and defiance, but the dignity and regal bearing associated with kings. Caratacus certainly did not make the magnificent speeches attributed to him by ancient historians; they wrote for a public who were as eager for drama and sensation as today's readers, and they did not hesitate to invent suitably stirring speeches to add to their narrative. What presumably happened in real life is that the British leader somehow impressed his captors, either with words or deeds. The general impression conveyed to those who witnessed Caratacus's visit to Rome (which did not include either Tacitus or Cassius Dio) was one of a man used to leading and commanding others and to being obeyed, a man who did not cower before the emperor.

These are the qualities for which Caratacus is remembered, and these are the qualities to which Welsh leaders aspired when they gave or took the name 'Caradog'. Their eagerness to identify with him has sometimes led to confusion. For example, Caradog ap Ynyr, sometimes called Caradog Freichfras ('Caradog Strong-Arm'), a fifth-century king of Gwent mentioned in the *Life of St Tathyw* and associated with the Roman sites of Caerwent and Caerleon, has also been linked with Caer Caradoc, which is of quite the wrong archaeological period. We have to take great care not to place too much credence in the words of medieval historians, whilst recognizing that there may be a grain of truth behind the stories they tell. They are even more inclined to romance and invention than their predecessors in Roman times.

Somewhere into this morass of legend and fact fits King Arthur, the ultimate Christian hero, who is mentioned in the early British pseudo-histories, but whose origins are not entirely clear. Despite the knowledge that Wales as an entity did not exist in the early post-Roman period, the idea that Arthur himself was Welsh will not go away. We will see, in subsequent chapters, the far-reaching influence of this perception.

From the time the Roman legions deserted Britannia in the late fourth century AD, we know the names of many Welsh rulers and quite a lot about some individuals. This is largely due to the preservation of the Celtic Christian tradition in Wales, carrying along with it the tradition of monastic learning. The *De Excidio Britanniae*, a work by the sixth century 'saint' Gildas, begins with a brief history of Roman Britain, and goes on to criticize contemporary rulers such as Maelgwn Gwynedd (who is believed to have reigned during the 520s) for failing to live up to the moral standards expected of a king. According to Gildas, Maelgwn committed treason, murder and adultery. The same ruler is mentioned in several other medieval manuscripts, where, though recognized as a wicked man, he is accorded some degree of respect for his achievements. Gildas explains this by pointing out that Maelgwn was a patron of many bards, whose sole purpose in life was to praise him.

Among the other sources for early British history are the *Historia Brittonum* and the *Annales Cambriae*. The *Historia Brittonum* was written in the ninth century, and is attributed to a monk named Nennius, whose exact identity is doubtful. The *Annales Cambriae* is believed to have been produced in the tenth century, but covers the years 447–954. It was written at the command of Owain ap Hywel (d.987), king of Deheubarth, a son of Hywel Dda. Finally, of course, we have the *Brut y Tywysogion*, which deals with Welsh royal doings from the year 682 right up to 1332. The date of its original composition is uncertain, as it is thought to be a translation of a lost Latin work entitled *Cronica Principium Wallie*, which was in turn based on the annals kept by Christian monasteries, specifically the Cistercian abbey of Strata Florida in Ceredigion.

## RULING MEDIEVAL WALES

The Welsh rulers whose names are recorded by history tend to be those who stood out among their peers in some way. Most Welshmen, even princes, were known by patronymics, a practice that does not assist the historian in attempting to differentiate between them. Rhodri Mawr ('the great') and his grandson, Hywel Dda ('the good'), are among the few who were given nicknames that reflected their achievements. Rhodri's father, Merfyn Frych ('the freckled') (d.844) is thought to have originated from the Isle of Man, another Celtic kingdom. Rhodri himself had the task of seeing off the Viking marauders who threatened the coast of Wales throughout the ninth and tenth centuries.

Rhodri was a true warrior-king, who met his death in battle. Hywel Dda, on the other hand, gained much of his territorial advantage by shrewd allegiances. Hywel's success as a ruler manifests itself in the coins of his reign that survive. He had them minted at Chester, which demonstrates the absence of any fear of the English on his part.

Morgan Hen ('the old'), a king of Morgannwg (d.975) can be assumed to have gained his nickname as a result of his longevity, and longevity was a prized thing at a time when life expectancy in Britain was around thirty. Staying alive might in itself have been enough to enable a ruler to stay on his throne, but the nickname may have an additional connotation of wisdom and experience.

Gruffydd ap Llywelyn (c.1007–63) is perhaps an exception to the rule that the most successful Welsh kings acquired nicknames. Gruffydd overcame several military setbacks to maintain and extend his hold on power. His reputation for aggression eclipsed even his reputation as a king, yet he remains known by a patronymic. This seems to demonstrate that a warlike nature was then, as it is now, far from being the only quality the Welsh admired in a ruler.

Owain Gwynedd (c.1100–70), a direct descendant of Rhodri Mawr, was one of the most successful all-round rulers Wales has ever known, so much so that his 'nickname' is the name of his kingdom. Owain personified Gwynedd, at a time when it was strong enough to take the greatest aggression the Normans could offer and retain its independence. Without his presence, Wales might quickly have disappeared from the map altogether.

If there is a more prestigious epithet than Owain's, it is the one applied to his nephew, Rhys ap Gruffydd (1132–97), known to the Welsh simply as 'Yr Arglwydd Rhys' and to the English as 'The Lord Rhys'. Rhys established himself firmly in Deheubarth after the death of his mother, Gwenllian, and two of his brothers, during the 1136 rebellion centred in Ceredigion.

## THE ROYAL CHARACTER

The term 'royal', in the English language, means 'relating to a king'. In the Welsh language, the equivalent term is 'brenhinol', which has exactly the same connotation. What does this mean? What does it take to be kingly?

It was important to the Welsh to have leaders whose power was absolute and unquestioned. Hence the Roman emperor Magnus Maximus (d.388) passed into folklore as 'Macsen Wledig' ('Wledig' meaning 'land-owning') through the Mabinogion. The real-life Maximus was a Celt from the Iberian peninsula, making him all the more interesting to those who recognized his ethnic connection with Wales. The grain of truth that no doubt lies within the folk tale of *Breuddwyd Macsen Wledig* (The Dream of Macsen Wledig) was emphasized by its author because it was seen as a subject for pride that an emperor, immigrant though he was, should have taken a bride from among the native people. That a Welsh princess should have become consort of such a huge empire was viewed as an achievement for Wales as a whole.

What had been tribes in Celtic times gradually developed into self-governing regions. Their rulers were known by various titles, including 'brenin' (king) and 'tywysog' (prince). 'Tywysog' has its roots in the verb 'tywys' ('to lead') and words of similar origin appear in other Celtic languages, notably 'Taoiseach', the title given to the prime minister of Ireland. 'Brenin' seems to have replaced another Welsh word, 'rhi', derived from the Latin 'rex', and to be etymologically connected with the name of the tribe dominant in the region in pre-Roman times, the Brigantes.

The most prominent of these petty kingdoms were Powys, Gwynedd, Seisyllwg, Dyfed, Brycheiniog, Morgannwg and Gwent. Who were these early Welsh royal families and how did they arrive at their positions of absolute, if territorially limited, power? It seems clear from the use of the word 'tywysog' that leadership was one of the main things the people sought from their rulers; but there was much more to it than that.

The Normans did not invent the feudal system, any more than the English invented the class system. Since Roman times, or perhaps even earlier, Welsh society had been developing its own pecking order, founded primarily on the ownership of land; this was the only kind of wealth and power that endured. Wales being a small country, its sub-kingdoms and principalities even smaller and its agricultural land poorer, the hierarchy was correspondingly reduced. Whilst it may seem to have been a society of near-equals, compared with today's experience, this was not really the case. The 'uchelwr' (a word which carries the combined connotations of 'landowner', 'nobleman' and 'administrator') was the wielder of power on a day-to-day basis. These were the people who ran Wales in the Middle Ages. If the land could be kept in the family, they might retain their power for many generations.

The correspondence between material possessions and earthly power is self-evident, but the rulers of Wales were also strongly associated with its religious life. Kings and queens were often regarded as saints, and vice versa. When Magnus Maximus was deposed and killed in 388, his Welsh widow, Elen, is said to have returned to Wales with her two sons, Cystennin and Publicius, and all three became regarded as saints. It seems fairly certain that there was confusion over their identity; it is easy to see how Elen may have become conflated with St Helena, mother of the Emperor Constantine. For some, Magnus Maximus himself, an orthodox Christian emperor who persecuted the Pelagian heretics, acquired the image of a martyr.

This view of kings as religious leaders as well as political and military ones is especially common in the early Middle Ages. Even St David seems to have played a part in politics. David (or Dewi Sant as he is known in Welsh) was one of the most vociferous opponents of the Pelagian heresy which swept Britain in the fifth and sixth centuries. At Llanddewibrefi, legend has it that he called a synod to refute the heresy, which rejected the concept of original sin. In the course of his keynote speech, it is said that the ground beneath his feet formed itself into a small hill in order that the crowd might be able to see and hear him better, and a white dove descended on his shoulder. Dewi's efforts to maintain the authority of the church help to explain why this 'miracle' is recorded and why he was officially canonized by the pope in 1123. The irony is that Pelagius, the originator of the heresy he so condemned, was also a Celt, and probably British.

Dewi Sant was himself of royal blood, albeit illegitimate. According to his eleventh-century biographer, Rhigyfarch, Dewi's father was a king of Ceredigion. He is described by Rhigyfarch as 'Sanctus rex ceredigionis', which may equally well mean 'Sanctus, the king of Ceredigion' or 'the holy king of Ceredigion'. There does not seem to have been anything very holy about Dewi's father, at least not to begin with. Dewi's mother, Non, was a nun or religious recluse, who was raped by the king of Ceredigion, and it was from this most unsanctified union that the saint was conceived. Whether this ancestry was invented, either in order to give the saint royal status or the other way round, will never be known. It is said that Non later married the king, but probably only after she had given birth to her son. The delivery is said to have taken place on top of a cliff in the middle of a storm, and the spot is marked by a much later building known as St Non's Chapel.

Dewi Sant is almost the only one of the leading figures of the period of Welsh history sometimes called the Age of the Saints to have been genuinely canonized. Other royal families of Wales also claimed descent from 'saints' or holy men, but few of them are in the same class. Brychan, who gave his name to the kingdom of Brycheiniog, lived in the fifth century. He was of Irish origin and is commemorated by place names throughout the Celtic world, in Ireland, Cornwall, Wales and Brittany. Like Dewi Sant's father, 'Saint' Brychan was a rapist, not to mention a polygamist, and fathered an estimated sixty-three children. His descendants form one of the three so-called 'tribes of the saints', the other two being those of Caw and Cunedda.

By far the most notable of these early rulers was Cunedda (d.c.460), and his reputation rests on his military successes, not on his devotion to God. Like Magnus Maximus before him, he was given the epithet 'Wledig', in recognition of the extent of the territories over which he ruled. It has been postulated that it was Magnus Maximus himself who invited Cunedda to Wales, in order that the stable regime maintained by the Romans should be sustained, at least in this western region, relatively safe from the depredations of Saxon invaders.

The eagerness shown by later rulers to trace their ancestry back to Cunedda is indicative of the respect in which his name continued to be held throughout the Middle Ages. The astonishing thing about Cunedda (for us in the twenty-first century, that is) is that he began his career in what is now Scotland. There being no significant ethnic difference between the Celtic tribes of mainland Britain at this time, he had no hesitation in relocating his power base when the Irish threatened to invade, despite the distances involved.

The land and people of Manaw Gododdin, immortalized in a poem (one of the earliest in the Welsh language) attributed to the bard Aneirin, is thought to have been located in the region of modern-day Clackmannanshire. In around 600, its leaders fought the Angles at a place referred to as 'Catraeth' in the north of England, tentatively identified as Catterick in North Yorkshire. Aneirin's poem influenced later royal bards, such as the prince-poet Owain Cyfeiliog (c.1130–97), not to mention Dafydd Benfras, whose works in praise of Llywelyn Fawr (c.1173–1240) draw heavily on the same tradition.

The evidence for Cunedda's existence is largely circumstantial; for that of his sons, even more so. According to legend, he had eight or nine of these, including such familiar names as Meirion and Ceredig, and Cunedda's kingdom was shared between them. Historians tend to believe that at least some of the names of Cunedda's sons were invented by later generations to give greater credibility to dynastic claims on the territories in question, particularly Ceredigion.

Cunedda's 'royalness' is unquestioned by later writers. Royalty feeds off royalty, and lineage was everything in the Middle Ages. The son of a ruler could normally expect to succeed him. The main difference among the Celts from the system we know today is that they did not practise primogeniture, but preferred what seems to our modern eyes a more even-handed system. All the king's sons, however many there were, and regardless of whether they were legitimate, could expect to inherit an equal share in his realm.

This system had its drawbacks. The in-fighting between a man's sons to control his property led inevitably to a dilution of the image of royal dignity attributed to them purely by their birth (important as that undoubtedly was). However, we may assume that the ability to overcome opposition was another aspect of kingship that was seen as admirable or at any rate 'regal' in the widest sense. At any rate, the experience of previous generations did not stop kings from procreating at a sometimes alarming rate, Owain Gwynedd being a notable example.

One consequence of the practice of primogeniture was that English kings expected a lot of their eldest sons. It did not matter whether a younger son was stronger, tougher or brighter than the eldest; there was no option to designate him heir to the throne. The Welsh did not have quite the same problem, and sons were thus able to develop according to their own abilities. If one son killed all the others in order to acquire the whole of his father's property, it might be regarded by many as morally reprehensible, but he did not find his rule challenged on the grounds that he had usurped the throne.

In England, a son was expected to live up to his father's example, and many were unable to do so: Edward II, Richard II and Henry VI would all fail miserably in the eyes of their subjects. Each would lose his hold on the kingdom as a result. As for daughters, they were fit for only one thing: to be married off to a potential ally. Elizabeth of Rhuddlan (1282–1316), the eighth daughter of Edward I, born in Wales during her father's successful campaign, eventually married a Marcher lord, Humphrey de Bohun, fourth earl of Hereford. She passed on her blood to her Welsh-born great-great-grandson King Henry V, making him royal several times over.

The Welsh had alternative expectations of their rulers. Piety was one of these, just as it had been for the Romans; but, as we have seen, it was a piety that had a host of manifestations. The English were not without religious devotion, and expected some sign of it from their rulers. Edward I, like his great-uncle Richard the Lionheart, fulfilled public expectations by going on crusade. Failure to live up to the standards required could lead to excommunication, as it had done for King John, whose subjects were encouraged to rise up against him by Pope Innocent III in 1209. This had given an unexpected opportunity to Llywelyn Fawr (c.1173–1240), prince of Gwynedd and most of Wales, who, despite being the king's son-in-law, took his chance and allied himself with some of John's disgruntled barons.

Thirty years later, Llywelyn, who had suffered a stroke, went into retirement at the Cistercian abbey of Aberconwy which he had founded. Such a retreat from the world would have been unthinkable for a Norman king of England, but was not without precedent in medieval Wales. (It might of course be argued that the Welsh princes had less to give up, and remained closer to the seat of power even after their retreat.) Princes such as Owain Cyfeiliog had found withdrawal from their role in government an attractive option. In 1195, Owain had retired to the abbey of Strata Marcella, leaving Powys in the hands of his son. No one thought any the less of him for it; indeed, his memory was revered, because Owain had not only been an effective ruler, he had been a poet.

Culture was another requirement in the repertoire of the successful king. One of the most beloved of Welsh princes was Hywel ab Owain Gwynedd, who has gone down in historical legend as a successful military leader, an upright man and a great poet. Some of Hywel's work has survived. His best-known offering, *Gorhoffedd Hywel ab Owain Gwynedd*, was a propaganda effort on behalf of his father, praising Gwynedd for its scenery (and its women). Hywel's death at the hands of his half-brothers led to his acquiring a saintly image and the possibly undeserved reputation of a lost leader who might have exceeded his father's achievements.

The Welsh medieval rulers were noted for their patronage of bards. This was in common with much of Europe. While England was in the grip of the so-called 'Dark Ages', the Welsh boasted poets of the stature of Taliesin and Aneirin. The Saxon king Alfred the Great hired a Welsh bishop, Asser, to improve his Latin and act as his official biographer. It has been suggested that Alfred might, in common with many of his fellow-countrymen, have been fluent in Welsh, but it is more likely that he conversed with Asser in Latin, the international language of literature and learning.

Naturally, the main purpose of keeping a household bard was to sing the praises of the man who held court. Another of the bard's functions was similar to that fulfilled by what we would now call a herald. The bard could recite the full genealogy of his prince, proving his calibre as a ruler by reference to his royal blood. This would become even more important from the fourteenth century onwards, when the Normans had become dominant but noble families still wished to underline their descent from indigenous Welsh rulers. In post-conquest Wales, it was through the oral tradition that the spirit of independence would be not only kept alive but propagated.

It seems clear that learning and culture were more highly sought-after qualities in a ruler of Wales than in the contemporary rulers of countries that had not been under Roman rule or had subsequently been invaded by 'barbarians'. It was only in the ninth century that the rulers of the English kingdoms seriously began to concern themselves with the arts. As for the Norman kings, they were too concerned with the consolidation of their military gains to pay much attention to cultural matters, and in any case they spoke and wrote a different language from the majority of their subjects.

In 1176, the Lord Rhys held a festival of music and poetry at his court in Cardigan. This is one of the first recorded eisteddfodau. The tradition of the chairing of bards goes back at least this far in the history of Wales, giving the lie to the popular misconception that the eisteddfod is a nineteenth-century invention. Even if the idea originally came from France or Ireland and was adapted to suit the Welsh, the basic shape of the festival is probably a thousand years old.

The lack of any female names in the historic catalogue of Welsh rulers is irrefutable evidence that royal women were seen in a different light from their fathers, brothers and sons. It was not a woman's rule to lead her people, however royal her birth. The pre-Roman Celts are known to have had queens, such as Cartismandua of the Brigantes and Boudicca of the Iceni, but these were both married women. Boudicca inherited her kingdom from her husband, and we have no idea how Cartismandua came by hers. They are certainly the exception rather than the rule.

Kingship could, however, be inherited through the female line, and many of the early Welsh rulers extended their territories through intermarriage with the female heirs of kings who had no sons of their own. In the early ninth century, Merfyn Frych of Gwynedd married Nest, a princess of Powys, giving their son, Rhodri Mawr, a springboard from which to establish his rule over most of Wales. Nearly a century later, Hywel Dda married a princess named Elen, enabling him to add Dyfed to his own kingdom of Seisyllwg, creating the territory known as Deheubarth.

If the maintenance of law and order was seen as a kingly duty, Hywel Dda was the epitome of the king. Not only did he codify the Welsh laws, he even issued his own coinage, manufactured in a mint at Chester. Hywel was well travelled, having in 928 completed the journey to Rome to which all western Christians aspired. In the Eternal City he was hailed as 'King of Wales'. Hywel was a skilled diplomat, however, and was prepared to do homage to Athelstan, king of England (d.939), to underline his right to rule. His relationship with his contemporaries over the border was such that his reign was unquestioned. Following his agreement with Athelstan, no battles between the English and the Welsh are recorded, and charters show that Welsh rulers attended the Englishman's court as 'subreguli'. Some time between 930 and 945, Hywel called an assembly at Whitland, and put together a document summarizing the laws of Wales as they then stood.

One thing to be said in favour of small kingdoms is that they do not require a great deal of administration. Subjects might receive near-personal attention from their ruler; they could certainly expect to see him from time to time. Is this what so many people resent about the modern monarchy? Does the collective memory of English, Welsh, Scottish and Irish alike go back far enough to yearn for the days when their rulers had time for them as individuals? Is this in fact a historical justification for the trend towards devolution?

Hywel Dda's attempt to bring his kingdom under the rule of law shows that he was concerned about the possibility of such a large territory becoming unwieldy and difficult to govern. In this he was ahead of his contemporaries, even in the larger Saxon kingdoms – except, perhaps, for Athelstan, whom he supported when the latter was challenged by the Scots during the 930s. The poem known as *Armes Prydein* is thought by some to have been written during Hywel's reign, and reflects the discontent of the Welsh under the dominance of the Saxons. It speaks of an alliance of the Celtic peoples of Britain and Ireland against Athelstan, and bemoans the latter's victory. This was a battle in which the Welsh seem to have taken no part, and which probably took place on England's northern borders, with the threat coming from the north rather than the west.

Following Hywel's death, his kingdom was broken up and divided between his three sons, whilst the other territories he had amassed returned to their original ruling families. Owain ap Hywel certainly had some awareness of his father's legacy, and is thought to have been responsible for the compilation of the *Annales Cambriae*, a chronicle of events in Wales and the wider world. In one manuscript it is immediately followed by a statement of Owain's pedigree. This may signify a sense of inadequacy, a need to emphasize Owain's right to rule by reference to his ancestors. At first he had shared the kingdom of Deheubarth with his brothers Edwin and Rhodri, but even between the three of them they had been unable to retain their hold on Gwynedd. Owain outlived his brothers by thirty years, passing the whole of Deheubarth to his son Maredudd (d.999).

Resilience and longevity were qualities that the Welsh might have valued, on the rare occasions they experienced them. With stability came peace and prosperity, and this was the best that the common people could hope for. Much as they admired a king who could exert his will on others by force, they admired him still more if he could hold on to his gains. Such a king was Gruffydd ap Cynan (*c*.1055–1137), father of the better-known Owain Gwynedd.

The English chronicler Orderic Vitalis referred to Gruffydd as 'rex Guallorum' ('king of the Welsh'), revealing that the English also recognized him as royal. His biography, written by a near-contemporary in the Welsh language, has survived, and tells a remarkable story. It is the story of a man who was so determined to rule Gwynedd that he conquered it no fewer than four times. The son of a Welsh prince and an Irish Viking princess, Gruffydd was around 20 when he made his first attempt on the throne of Gwynedd. He was joined in his invasion attempt by none other than Robert of Tilleul, a Norman adventurer with a particularly bloodthirsty reputation who saw some advantage in a temporary alliance with the youth. The Norman later became known as Robert of Rhuddlan, after the stronghold he established on licence from William the Conqueror. Although Gruffydd successfully seized much of the territory he wanted, he was unable to hold onto it, and was forced to retreat to Ireland. Five years later, he was back, this time in an alliance with Rhys ap Tewdwr (d.1093), displaced ruler of Deheubarth. At the Battle of Mynydd Carn in 1081, the allies defeated all their enemies and regained their respective kingdoms.

Shortly after this second conquest of Gwynedd, Gruffydd ap Cynan was taken prisoner by the Normans. He remained in captivity for at least twelve years. The story goes that the prisoner was on show, in the market-place at Chester, in chains, when a local man, Cynwrig Hir ('Cynwrig the Tall'), carried him off. If Gruffydd owed his freedom to Cynwrig, he nevertheless had already shown his powers of endurance, and his long sojourn in prison seems only to have made him more determined. Yet again, he was unable to hold on to Gwynedd and fled once more to Ireland; but a couple of years later he was back, and this time there was no question of his superiority over his rivals. Robert of Rhuddlan, who had betrayed his former ally, was later killed trying to repel a sea attack by Gruffydd's raiders, and the Norman's severed head was displayed on the mast of their ship. With such a history, it is no wonder Gruffydd's life was recorded and held up as an example to his successors. Tenacity and perseverance, then, should be added to the list of qualities admired in a Welsh ruler.

As far as political skill and diplomacy go, though, it would be difficult to find a more successful Welsh prince than the Lord Rhys. In September 1171, Rhys had a formal meeting with King Henry II in the Forest of Dean, and the two entered a non-aggression pact whereby Rhys would pay annual tribute to the English king; Henry in return agreed to enter Wales only for the purposes of transporting troops to Ireland. Henry even turned a blind eye when Rhys failed to deliver the promised tribute. The frequent absences from the kingdom of Henry's successor, King Richard I, gave Rhys the opportunity he needed to expand and consolidate. He and his sons had just completed another successful campaign against the Normans in 1197 when the Lord Rhys died suddenly, of a 'pestilence' that was ravaging the country. Although he had been excommunicated as a result of a falling out with the Norman bishop of St David's, he was buried in the cathedral there, in full recognition (according to *Brut y Tywysogion*) of his status as 'unconquered head of all Wales'.

## SON OF PROPHECY

By the thirteenth century, there was something else the Welsh were looking for. They awaited the 'mab darogan' or 'son of prophecy', who would come to save them from the English yoke. Saxon or Norman, English rulers were all much the same as far as the Welsh were concerned. The concept of 'mab darogan' is credited to Myrddin, better known to us as Merlin, a mystical figure linked with the legend of Arthur. The first recorded use of the term, however, is in a poem addressed to Llywelyn Fawr by his bard, Prydydd y Moch. Prydydd says that this Messianic figure will be 'o hil eryron o Eryri', a descendant of the eagles of Snowdonia, suggesting the royal family of Gwynedd. Llywelyn had more sense than to claim the title of 'mab darogan' for himself; better to leave that implicit in the words of his bard.

A hundred years later, one of Llywelyn's dispossessed descendants, Owain Lawgoch (*c*.1330–78), would be recognized by his followers as the son of prophecy and would make a serious but unsuccessful attempt to invade Wales in 1372. Owain Lawgoch was assassinated shortly afterwards, but within thirty years another would-be claimant had arisen.

It was alleged by some that Owain Glyndŵr (*c*.1359–*c*.1416) ate eagles' flesh to make himself worthy of his people's expectations. The prospects looked bright for a few years, until the advent of a brighter star, Henry of Monmouth, who destroyed Glyndŵr's plans for the renewal of Wales's independence.

The Welsh had to wait until 1485 for their true Messiah, but when Henry Tudor came along, there was no longer any doubt. Born in Pembroke and carrying the royal blood of England, Wales and France, Tudor had been the subject of a prophecy made by his uncle, King Henry VI, who had by some psychic or magical power recognized the boy as a future king. Snatching the throne, in a shrewd but violent manner, from the usurper Richard III, Henry Tudor proceeded to establish a dynasty that would rule England and Wales for over a hundred years and make the country an international superpower. The search for the son of destiny seemed to be at an end.

# Normans

The Normans invaded England in 1066, but did not attempt to take Wales at that point. They preferred a piecemeal approach, and within ten years, William the Conqueror had created three new earldoms along the Welsh 'march', the border land that kept the Welsh and English apart. Hitherto it had been difficult to tell where England ended and Wales began. The border populations spoke both languages, and England up to now had been, like Wales, less of a nation than a collection of petty kingdoms. The new earls of Hereford, Chester, Shrewsbury and, later, Gloucester, were loyal to the new ruling dynasty of England, and recognized it as their duty to subdue Wales on behalf of the Norman kings.

Some of the Norman lords began stealthily, lulling the Welsh into a false sense of security through marriage alliances. Others immediately embarked on an expansionist strategy, building castles and raiding Welsh territory. It was not until 1081 that King William himself first entered Wales. William claimed to be on a pilgrimage to St David's, but he had other motives. Along with the government of England, he had taken on its church, and to emphasize his control of the kingdom's spiritual life, he had installed his mentor, Lanfranc, former abbot of Caen, as archbishop of Canterbury. While at St David's, the king took the opportunity to ensure that its bishop knew his place and recognized the authority of Canterbury. (There would not be an archbishop of Wales until 1920, the year in which the Church of England in Wales was finally disestablished, disendowed and replaced with its independent Welsh counterpart.)

Needless to say, William was as interested in the secular life of his kingdom as in the spiritual. His journey into Wales was an opportunity to make a show of power and to put fear into the hearts of the local population. Rhys ap Tewdwr, ruler of Deheubarth, was prepared to pay William £40 a year protection money in order to keep his own little kingdom. (Significantly, this was the same amount paid to the king by the Norman lord Robert of Rhuddlan to retain *his* territories in north Wales.) More important than the financial incentive, in symbolic terms, was the 'homage' William obtained from the Welsh ruler. The Norman tradition was a ceremony in which the vassal would kneel bareheaded before his lord and pledge his loyalty. As a result, not only did the vassal owe service to his new overlord, but in return he could expect the support of that lord in times of trouble.

The Marcher lords who were too timorous to venture into Wales sometimes delegated their responsibilities to their own vassals, lesser lords such as Eustace de Cruer, who is credited with the building of the first castle at Mold. Eustace was granted the lordship of Mold by King William II, son of the Conqueror, but the territory was by no means firmly in Norman hands. Some fifty years later, when the original castle had been upgraded by Robert de Montalt, Owain Gwynedd seized it, and in 1149, at Consyllt, he gave the Norman earl of Chester, Ranulf de Gernon, a bloody nose when the latter tried to take back 'his' territory. At some stage, the English got their castle back, but kept it only until 1198, when Owain's grandson Llywelyn Fawr retrieved it and held it. Mold Castle remained a bone of contention in 1245, when Llywelyn's son, Dafydd (d.1246), was ordered to give it up to the Norman 'seneschal' of Chester. Dafydd refused and the dispute continued. In 1263 that hardy prince of Powys, Gruffydd ap Gwenwynwyn (d.1286), destroyed the castle, symbolic as it was of English dominance. By 1302 it had been rebuilt by the English and was the recognized property of the new 'prince of Wales', the future Edward II. In 1322 it was again being besieged by a Welsh rebel, this time Sir Gruffydd Llwyd, the very man who is reputed to have brought Edward I the news of his son's birth at Caernarfon Castle. Five years later it passed into the hands of Queen Isabella, regent of England and the mother of King Edward III.

The history of Mold Castle typifies the struggle for supremacy in the Welsh Marches, particularly in the north, where the landscape was more hostile to English armies. In 1114, Henry I invaded Gwynedd and Powys, but he did not stay there. He was more successful in the south, where he made other conquests, apparently including Princess Nest (d.c.1136), the daughter of that same Rhys ap Tewdwr who had been prepared to pay homage to Henry's father. As a result, Nest is said to have given birth to a son, Henry Fitzroy (1103–58). Both King Henry and Princess Nest developed far-from-spotless reputations in the bedroom department, and it seems safe to assume that she was a willing partner in the liaison (if it really happened).

It was not only in the Marches that the struggle between the Normans and the natives went on. As the king of England effectively controlled the activities of the church, his influence continued to be felt as far west as Pembrokeshire. Henry I issued a 'charter of privileges' to St David's, conferring the status of a town on the tiny settlement which just happened to have a very important cathedral. He may have believed it would have a civilizing effect. The town became a centre of pilgrimage, and the residents could not pick and choose who should be allowed access to the shrine of St David. Two visits here were the equivalent of one to Rome, and naturally the English were among the most frequent visitors.

Henry's policy towards Wales, copied by the more effective English kings and a strategy that eventually worked well for Edward I, was 'divide and rule'. When he saw an opportunity to interfere between two Welsh princes who were at one another's throats, Henry would take it. Yet his incursions into Wales were designed to inspire awe and fear in the natives, rather than to take administrative control. He had no use for Wales as another region to govern; he merely wished to ensure its continued subservience.

In 1138, Henry's successor Stephen created the earldom of Pembroke for his retainer Gilbert de Clare, making it clear that he regarded Welsh estates as being in the gift of the king of England, regardless of what the locals might have to say about the matter. Stephen, however, was already engulfed in civil war, as Henry's legitimate daughter, Matilda, tried to regain the kingdom her father had willed to her. The king had no time to spare for the conquest of Wales, and this was one of the keys to Owain Gwynedd's ability to rule north Wales, virtually unchallenged, for so long, and to expand southwards into Ceredigion, taking control of it back from the Normans. Owain was the most notable of several native rulers who took advantage of 'the Anarchy' to strengthen their own positions.

During this twelve-year period of 'anarchy', no one was quite sure who ruled England. This is not to say that the Welsh took no part in the conflict. One knight who had a major role in the civil war was Robert of Gloucester (d.1147), also called Robert of Caen, whom some have identi- fied as the child of Henry I by Nest though it is generally believed that his mother was Sybilla Corbet. As lord of Glamorgan, Robert of Gloucester had his power base in south Wales, and it was to him that the care of the deposed duke of Normandy, Robert Curthose (elder brother of Henry I), had fallen; Curthose was a prisoner in Cardiff Castle from 1126 until his death in 1134. At Cardiff Robert of Gloucester went so far as to mint coins in the name of his half-sister Matilda, whose claim to the throne he loyally supported. Robert had achieved peace in his part of the Marches by making treaties with local Welsh rulers, and was well regarded, for a Norman. He had many Welshmen in his service, as did the earl of Chester, Ranulf, when they jointly defeated King Stephen at Lincoln in 1141.

Henry II, grandson of Henry I, repeated the attempt at Welsh dom- inance in 1157, to be met with resistance by Owain Gwynedd, that most able of Welsh leaders. The two reached an uneasy settlement by which Henry gained Rhuddlan and some other territories and undertook not to trouble Owain again. The peace did not last, and Owain took back what he had lost in the course of the next decade. In 1165, at the Battle of Crogen near Chirk, Welsh chroniclers proudly report that Henry, accompanied by 'a host beyond number of the picked warriors of England and Normandy and Flanders and Gascony and Anjou and all the North and Scotland', was defeated by an alliance of princes that included both Owain Gwynedd and Owain Cyfeiliog. Henry's last attempt at invasion was defeated by the Welsh weather.

In 1174, however, Owain's son, Dafydd, married Henry's half-sister, Emma of Anjou, in an attempt to bring the royal houses closer together and prevent further bloodshed. Emma was illegitimate, the daughter of Geoffrey of Anjou by a mistress. For the Welsh, illegitimacy held no stigma. As far as the royal court of Gwynedd was concerned, Emma was a princess. Henry's son, King John, would later repeat the experiment, marrying his own illegitimate daughter to Dafydd's nephew.

Whatever the relationship between Henry II and Wales, he needed to travel through the country in order to reach Ireland, another independent land on which the Norman kings had designs. Henry embarked at the port now known as Milford Haven in 1172. An advance army had already prepared the ground, including many Welshmen; they were led by Richard de Clare, nominal earl of Pembroke, known to history as 'Strongbow'.

It was in 1188, during the latter part of Henry II's reign, that Gerald of Wales (alternatively called 'Giraldus Cambrensis' in Latin and 'Gerallt Cymro' in Welsh) made his famous journey through the land. He travelled in the entourage of the archbishop of Canterbury, Baldwin of Exeter, on a campaign to recruit men for the Third Crusade. Gerald was a clergyman, of mixed Norman and Welsh blood. His grandmother was the notorious Nest, princess of Deheubarth and former mistress of King Henry I. Nest was sometimes known as 'the Helen of Wales' because of her ability to stir men to violence. The de Clares had obtained some of their west Wales lands from Henry I, when that king dispossessed his former allies, Cadwgan ap Bleddyn (1051–1111) and his son Owain, as a result of Owain's action in running off with Nest, thus shaming her Norman husband. Owain ap Cadwgan continued in the king's service, but this did not prevent Gerald of Windsor from pursuing him to his death in 1116. Angharad, Gerald's daughter by Nest, was the mother of Gerald of Wales.

Although he could claim royal blood on his Welsh side, Gerald was unsuccessful in his attempts to achieve the status of bishop. His rejection seems to have been based on his very Welshness, leading to his being considered potentially unreliable as an enforcer of the archbishop of Canterbury's edicts. Gerald was, however, close to the young king, serving

Henry II as chaplain; and he was the ideal choice as a companion and interpreter for Baldwin. He had indeed already accompanied Henry's son, Prince John, to Ireland in 1185.

The new archbishop of York, enthroned in 1189, was Geoffrey, an illegitimate son of the king. Gerald quickly became one of Geoffrey's staunchest supporters. When the archbishop's half-brother took the throne as King Richard I, both Geoffrey and Gerald fell out of favour. Gerald became more outspoken in his criticisms of secular authority, and his former relationship with Prince John did not enable him to obtain high office in the church even when John became king in 1199.

Although individual Englishmen were free to come and go within Wales, the country was considered dangerous in parts. Hills, forests and rivers were all hazards, and the language barrier did not help. In his *Descriptio Cambriae*, written in 1194, Gerald recommends to his monarch that the final conquest of Wales (which Henry II had recognized as being still a long way off) should be attempted only with men who knew the terrain. Only the Marches could provide such men, he warns, and even they would have difficulty with the guerrilla tactics employed by the Welsh. It would be better for the king of England to bide his time and rely on the continual internal divisions of the Welsh princes to weaken the opposition.

The stand-off continued into the reign of King John, who formed an alliance with Owain Gwynedd's grandson, Llywelyn Fawr ('the Great'). As in the previous generation, the alliance was cemented through marriage to an illegitimate princess, this time Joan, called Siwan by the Welsh. Joan's career as princess of Gwynedd is well known. Despite the period she spent under house-arrest after being caught with a lover, William de Braose, there is written evidence that she did, in the course of her life, succeed in helping to keep the peace between her husband and her father, and later between Llywelyn and her half-brother, King Henry III. Most importantly, she left a legitimate son who could succeed Llywelyn as prince.

The man to whom the earldom of Pembroke had passed, after the death of the great Marcher lord Richard de Clare, was William Marshal, de Braose's father-in-law. Marshal was a renowned soldier, called by some 'the greatest knight that ever lived'. Through his 1189 marriage to Isabel, the daughter of 'Strongbow', William Marshal came into possession of vast estates scattered through Ireland (where County Clare is named after his wife's family), England (where the village of Clare in Suffolk was named after their place of origin) and south Wales. Marshal played a leading role in the defeat of Rhys ap Gruffydd in 1192, and ten years later was made custodian of Cardigan castle by King John. He went on to appropriate the lordship of Emlyn from Maelgwn ap Rhys (c.1170–1230). In 1212, at the age of nearly 70, Marshal was still a leading figure in the campaign against the Welsh, this time joining the king to fight against the up-and-coming Welsh leader, Llywelyn Fawr. That he bore no personal hostility towards the Welsh is evinced by his voluntary return of two castles to Llywelyn as soon as peace terms were agreed.

Llywelyn wisely did not rely on his wife's family ties with the English monarchy. In 1212 (after his father-in-law, the king of England, had been excommunicated by the pope), Llywelyn wrote to the king of France, Philippe II, referring to an embassy he had received from that king. Llywelyn's letter promises that he and his heirs will ally themselves with Philippe and his heirs, having their friends and enemies in common. In return, he expects Philippe to recognize him as ruler of Wales. Although he refers to the other princes of Wales, it is very clear that Llywelyn considers himself their unchallenged leader, and regards their status as subservient to his own. He has a very clear sense of his own royalty.

By the time Llywelyn's career reached its apogee in the 1220s, William Marshal was dead. His son and namesake continued in loyalty to the English crown, and retook the castles of Cardigan and Carmarthen which his father had given up to Llywelyn. In this struggle against the prince of Gwynedd, Marshal junior allied himself with lesser Welsh princes, such as Cynan ap Hywel ap Rhys, who did not wish to be dominated by Gwynedd. (Cynan's reward was the lordship of Emlyn.) This reveals a more complex situation than we have been tempted to recognize by the age-old tales of English oppression. The reality was that the Welsh were answerable to no one ruler, and resistance to English domination (whether by individuals or by groups) had as much to do with that unwillingness to be controlled as it did to a hatred of the English.

Llywelyn, having outlived the second William Marshal, allied himself with the latter's son, Richard, when the new earl fell out with King John's successor, Henry III, during the 1230s. Between them, Richard Marshal and Llywelyn Fawr soon controlled the southern Welsh border. The areas not yet under the control of the Marcher lords were known, in Latin, as 'Pura Wallia', and Llywelyn controlled most of these, and indeed most of north Wales. The Peace of Middle, negotiated in 1234, ensured that Llywelyn retained firm control of his principality until the end of his life.

Llywelyn was in no awe of his brother-in-law the king, whom he had known from a small child. When, in 1230, Llywelyn's wife and Henry's half-sister Joan was discovered in a liaison with William de Braose, lord of Abergavenny, whom Llywelyn had entertained in good faith, de Braose was immediately executed by the cuckolded husband. After a brief banishment from court, Joan was forgiven and welcomed back into the marital home. Llywelyn genuinely loved her, but one might question whether he would have been so lenient had he not had to take into account the risk of offending the king of England. Not only did he allow Joan to resume her place at his side, but he allowed his son, Dafydd, to go ahead with the marriage that had already been arranged, to none other than de Braose's daughter, Isabella. Political alliances would seem to have taken precedence over personal feelings in this case. Many prefer to see this as a sign of Llywelyn's high-mindedness, in that he chose not to punish the daughter for the sins of the father, but no one bothered to record Isabella's feelings on the matter.

Llywelyn's action in selecting Dafydd as his heir, rather than his older, illegitimate son Gruffydd, reveals his willingness to compromise with the English. He saw that the future of Wales might depend on the country becoming more like its threatening neighbour, rather than continuing to resist the inevitable. He was not so wedded to Welsh law that he would champion the rights of his eldest son when he could use his younger son's Norman blood as a means of preserving Welsh independence. Llywelyn's strategy for assuring the succession proved not to be as watertight as he had hoped. Shortly after his death, Henry III recognized Dafydd, the legitimate son of Llywelyn and Joan, as 'prince of Wales'. He received the new prince's homage at Gloucester, and even set a coronet on his head. By the following year, however, relations had deteriorated and Henry invaded Gwynedd. Dafydd spent the rest of his short reign staving off the inevitable.

Dafydd died prematurely, six years after his father, leaving no heir. It was another Llywelyn, the son of Dafydd's illegitimate elder brother, Gruffydd, who eventually came to the fore in Gwynedd, dominating his own three brothers in the process. Picking up where his grandfather had left off, Llywelyn ap Gruffydd (c.1230–82) set out to become undisputed ruler of Wales, and was recognized as such in the Treaty of Montgomery, signed in 1267. With Henry III, now an immature adult, still on the English throne, Llywelyn's position was a strong one, threatened mainly by the petty jealousies of lesser Welsh princes. He had reached this position largely thanks to a timely alliance with Simon de Montfort, earl of Leicester, the powerful French-born baron who was determined to make the king more answerable to his subjects.

Simon's campaign for a parliament was deemed necessary because there were no real restrictions on the activities of the English kings. Their own Marcher lords were as vulnerable to their mood swings as the Welsh were. Even William Marshal had suffered from King John's tyranny, having his Welsh castles taken away from him in a fit of pique and then returned in a moment of greater sanity. In 1210, angry with his former favourite William de Braose (grandfather of the man who would cuckold Llywelyn Fawr), and even more angry when he discovered that the latter had run away to France to elude his displeasure, John took William's wife and his eldest son prisoner instead. Maud de Braose was a feisty woman, who had defended her husband's possession of Painscastle against Welsh attack during the 1190s. She had as good as called John a murderer after the mysterious death of his nephew, Arthur of Brittany, in 1203. Now John took his vengeance on her and her son. They died in captivity, perhaps at Windsor or at Corfe Castle in Dorset, starved to death on the king's orders. William de Braose senior, who had planned to be buried at Brecon, died in exile. The de Braoses, Norman to the core, nevertheless left their hearts in the Welsh border country.

Alliances between Welsh chieftains and Marcher lords were not uncommon, and, where they occurred, could produce a lethal cocktail of home-grown loyalties and imported military power that threatened the English throne. It was an alliance between Robert Fitzhamon (d.1107) and a local prince that had first given the Normans their power base in Glamorgan, and Henry I had imprisoned Iorwerth ap Bleddyn (1053–1111) for his alliance with the earl of Shrewsbury, Robert of Bellême, when the latter supported Robert Curthose, Henry's brother and rival for the throne.

Henry III's eldest son, the future King Edward I, disapproved of his father's vacillating rule, and was determined to show himself a strong ruler when the time came. It was Edward who put an end to Simon de Montfort's dominance, defeating the rebel barons at the Battle of Evesham in 1265 and banishing the entire de Montfort family from England. In doing so he was sending into exile his own aunt and his first cousins (Simon's widow being the sister of King Henry III). Simon was one of those progressive English barons who had allied themselves with the Welsh rather than make enemies of them. His pact with Llywelyn ap Gruffydd was cemented by Llywelyn's promise to marry Simon's daughter Eleanor, and this did not endear the Welsh leader to Prince Edward. Seven years after Evesham, Edward came to the throne. Having eliminated the internal opposition, he felt safe within the boundaries of England, and cast his eyes further afield.

By 1282, Edward I wanted Wales very badly. His reasons cannot have had a great deal to do with the natural resources of the principality. Geographically, Wales was a troublesome region, with its tendency to mountainous terrain, poor soil and generally wet weather. What it did have, in abundance, was a set of minor rulers who made Edward's hold on England less secure than it might otherwise have been. As long as they stayed on their side of the border and did not resist too strongly when his own barons infiltrated Welsh territory, he had been prepared to tolerate them. He had enough on his plate, with crusades and rebellious Scots leaders, to have no strong motive for an invasion of weak little Wales. Besides, it was only a matter of time before the barons did the job for him. The king did, however, feel obliged to make his dominance felt when he came up against a Welsh leader who was unwilling to lie down and be walked over.

It was the petty quarrel between Edward I and Llywelyn ap Gruffydd that escalated into internecine war, putting an end to Wales's 900-year-old tradition of independence from England. Edward was simply tired of waiting. The policy of delegating the conquest to the king's barons carried with it the danger of insubordination. Marcher lords must be made to share their profits with the monarch who had treated them so generously; they must not be allowed to become petty kings themselves. One of the great Marcher titles, the earldom of Chester, comprising Cheshire and Flintshire, its last incumbent having died in 1237, passed briefly into the hands of Simon de Montfort before his disgrace. Edward I himself, while heir to the throne, had briefly been known as 'Lord' of Chester, and he bestowed the earldom on his eldest son, with the result that princes of Wales from 1301 onwards have also been earls of Chester. The title makes a connection between the old and new regimes.

Llywelyn's marriage to Eleanor de Montfort was guaranteed to provoke the king of England. Edward had exiled his cousin along with the rest of her family, but the ostensible reason for his displeasure was that Llywelyn had not asked his permission to go ahead with the marriage. Moreover, the Welsh prince had tried to avoid giving Edward any say in the matter by having his bride brought to him by sea. The king, having got wind of the wedding plans, arranged for the ship to be taken by 'pirates', and Eleanor languished for more than two years under house arrest at Windsor until Llywelyn had made suitable concessions. The king then made a show of celebrating the marriage in fine style at Worcester Cathedral. At the very last moment, he extracted further concessions from the Welsh. He was determined to show Llywelyn who *really* ruled the country.

The death of Llywelyn ap Gruffydd, 'Llywelyn the Last' as he is called in English and, more tellingly, 'Ein Llyw Olaf' ('our last leader') in Welsh, is a defining moment in the history of Wales. It is in this event that lovers of Welsh independence see their nation subjugated by a foreign oppressor. In particular, the ignominy of Llywelyn's death (killed in an ambush and decapitated by a knight who had no idea of his royal status) seems to sum up the destruction of Welsh identity. King Edward, who accepted Llywelyn's head as a gift and paraded it around the streets of London, is regarded as no better than a murderer whose tyranny continued unchecked following the demise of the only leader with both the competence and the courage to stand against him.

Edward did not see himself as a tyrant but as a realist and a modernizer. He seems to have believed he was doing Wales a favour by subjugating it and annexing it to England. That he took his revenge on the Welsh and their leaders is not in dispute. The brutality with which he executed Llywelyn's younger brother Dafydd, the callousness with which he condemned Dafydd's small sons to life imprisonment (from which they never emerged), the sheer coldness of his decision to send the daughters of Dafydd and Llywelyn into convents for the rest of their lives, all testify to his determination to put down any opposition that might arise.

Yet his pronouncements are also evidence of a man who wanted to appear generous in victory and who placed some value on the new lands now made available to him. Edward claimed that his intention was not to punish the children of his enemies, merely to put an end to division and rule in peace. 'Having the Lord before our eyes, pitying also her sex and her age, that the innocent may not seem to atone for the iniquity and ill-doing of the wicked', he wrote, by way of excuse, to the abbot of Sempringham in 1283, shortly before dispatching the baby Gwenllian to spend the rest of her life with the Gilbertine order in far-off Lincolnshire.

What Edward had wanted, as much as anything, was to claim the land of Wales as a personal possession. Having been given all the royal estates in Wales as a coming-of-age present, he saw no reason why the rest of the country should not be administered in the same way. It stood to reason that his way of doing things (the Norman way) must be more efficient than the old-fashioned Welsh way, that the laws of England must be fairer than those of Wales, and that the Welsh would be better off under an English ruler.

Before very long, there was another Edward on the throne. Edward II consolidated the actions of his father in relation to Wales. He called Welsh representatives to Parliament, and even had them serving in his army against their Celtic cousins, the Scots (at that time still a separate nation). He was not without popularity in Wales, of which, as prince of Wales, he had been invested as nominal ruler in 1301. He had, after all, been born in Caernarfon. It was to Wales that Edward II went in 1326, when his wife Isabella and her lover, Roger Mortimer, rebelled and brought a huge French army from her native land to challenge his rule. His intention was to take refuge in the Welsh estates of his favourite, Hugh le Despenser.

It did him no good at all. The Welsh were not fond of the Despensers. Hugh and his father had acquired vast possessions within the principality, by virtue of advantageous marriages, royal favour and downright theft, and they were not regarded as good landlords. The locals might have been prepared to follow their king, but not if it meant saving the Despensers. In a spot now known as Pant-y-Brad ('glen of treachery'), King Edward II was captured by his enemies. He never sat on his throne again.

# Royal Blood

As we have seen, the quest for legitimacy through ancestry goes back to the earliest recorded history. In 855, Cyngen, former ruler of Powys, died at Rome, where he had gone on pilgrimage, perhaps as a refuge from the constant aggression of the princes of Gwynedd. Before leaving Wales, Cyngen had apparently erected the monument now known as the Pillar of Eliseg, which still stands near Valle Crucis Abbey in Denbighshire. The inscription, which has almost completely faded from view, was recorded by the great Welsh scholar Edward Lhuyd (1660–1790). It records the descent of Cyngen and his ancestors from both Vortigern, a prominent ruler of post-Roman Britain, and from the Roman emperor Magnus Maximus. Cyngen was in the process of being edged out of his kingdom, but he had staked his claim, and that of his family, on Powys. It was the marriage of Cyngen's daughter to Merfyn Frych that united the kingdoms under their son, Rhodri Mawr, and temporarily resolved the issue.

Genealogy was as popular in the seventeenth century as it is now, and Sir John Wynn of Gwydir (1553–1627), in his *History of the Gwydir Family*, made a point of emphasizing that his ancestry went back to Cunedda. Sir John evidently thought his Welsh royal blood as significant as ever, despite having lived through the reigns of Mary I and Elizabeth I, in which time he saw England and Wales confirmed as one state. Scotland was added in 1603 through the accession of James VI of Scotland to the English throne as James I. By the time Sir John died, the new young king, Charles I, still looked secure on the throne. Yet the merger of the three nations only seems to have increased the Wynns' pride in their descent from the ancient British ruling families.

Both the House of York and the House of Lancaster could claim direct descent from Llywelyn the Great. King Henry V acquired his Welsh royal blood through his mother, Mary de Bohun (d.1394). Mary's mother was Joan Fitzalan, a descendant of Roger Mortimer, lord of Wigmore (1231–82). Roger Mortimer's mother, Gwladus (d.1251), was a daughter of Llywelyn the Great – whether legitimate or illegitimate is uncertain. The Yorks, on the other hand, were descended from the only one of Llywelyn's daughters who is known to have been legitimate: Elen (d.1253), whose descendant, Joan of Kent (1328–85), married into the English royal family.

In 1361, Joan became the wife of the Black Prince, son of Edward III and grandson of the ill-fated Edward II, simultaneously becoming the first 'official' princess of Wales. Joan passed on her Welsh royal blood (much diluted) not only to her youngest son, King Richard II, but also to the children of an earlier marriage, her eldest son Thomas Holland and his younger brother John.

In the early days of Wales's subjugation to England, it might have been convenient for the new prince of Wales, Edward of Caernarfon, to trade on his Welsh birth. He did not, however, attempt to confer the title or the nominal responsibility for the principality on his own son, the future Edward III. There was no precedent, and Edward II saw no reason to do so. Perhaps he would eventually have done so if time had allowed; Edward III was only 15 when his father was deposed. A wiser and more accomplished king than his father, he saw a reason to continue with the tradition, and invested his own heir apparent, another Edward, as prince of Wales when the latter was only 13. It was a good move to give the youth some responsibility; by the time he was 16, he was commanding armies. The Black Prince and his wife (by virtue of her birth rather than any other association with the principality) would be associated with Wales even when they went to live in Aquitaine, where both their sons were born.

The Black Prince seems to have been regarded by the Welsh as a hard taskmaster and yet he was admired as a military leader, travelling to Chester to recruit archers from across the border for his campaigns in France. He 'ruled' Wales with the aid of a council of twelve chosen men, and set his seal on documents such as the charters of privileges issued to the towns of Nefyn and Pwllheli in 1355. At the same time, he took cynical advantage of his position to raise taxes for the pursuance of his military goals. In 1347 the diocese of St David's launched a ten-year court case against him for his failure to respect their status as non-payers. The church still had the ultimate power and privilege; in the Middle Ages this was the only institution that could challenge the heir to the throne and hope to get away with it.

Whereas the sickly Plantagenet strain died out with Richard II, the thriving Holland dynasty intermarried with everyone in sight, including the Plantagenets, the Beauforts and the Fitzalans. Their blood ran in the veins of Richard, duke of York, father of King Edward IV and grandfather of Elizabeth of York. When Elizabeth married Henry Tudor (himself descended from the Hollands), the result was a match made in heaven as far as the Welsh were concerned. Edward Parry, in his *Royal Visits and Progresses to Wales* (1850), describes Henry Tudor as 'the great restorer of the Royal Line of England', on the grounds not only of Henry's own direct descent from King Edward III, King Charles VI of France and Llywelyn the Great, but of his shrewd choice of bride.

If Henry Tudor's right to rule over Wales as well as England was recognized by the Welsh, that of some of his ancestors was not. Henry of Monmouth (the future Henry V), in particular, might have been admired in Wales for his military prowess, but as the son of a usurper, he met with strong resistance when representing his father during the rebellion of Owain Glyndŵr. Glyndŵr asserted his right to rule Wales in 1400, shortly after Henry Bolingbroke, duke of Lancaster, had seized the throne from the 'rightful' king, Richard II.

The description of Owain Glyndŵr as the 'Welsh prince of Wales' and Henry of Monmouth as the 'English prince of Wales' is somewhat misleading. Not only was Henry of Monmouth born in Wales but, through his mother, Mary de Bohun, he was a direct descendant of Llywelyn the Great. Owain, by contrast, could only claim descent on his father's side from the dynasty of Powys Fadog, and on his mother's from the Lord Rhys of Deheubarth. The irony is thus that, by any laws of inheritance we understand, the official prince of Wales had a better claim to the title than the 'true' 'Welsh' prince of Wales.

The significant difference was that Owain was descended through the male line and Henry through the female (his mother, through her mother, was descended from Llywelyn's daughter Gwladus). The Welsh barely acknowledged the female line. Kingdoms passed from father to son; failing that, they passed from father-in-law to son-in-law or from uncle to nephew. Women, as ever, were totally overlooked in the search for a successor.

# Welsh Pretenders: Owain Lawgoch and Owain Glyndŵr

∽

The revolt of Owain Glyndŵr is considered by many to be the single most important event in Welsh history. The folk memory of Owain's fifteenth-century parliaments at Machynlleth and Harlech has become a rallying-point for supporters of Welsh self-government. The 600th anniversary of the rebellion, in the year 2000, gave rise to celebrations and commemorative events of various kinds. It also resulted in the creation of an Owain Glyndŵr Society, with the initial aim of erecting a suitable memorial in Machynlleth.

The subsequent formation of a campaigning group, Senedd '04, was inspired by the anniversary of Glyndŵr's 1404 parliament, and is geared towards recreating the Machynlleth parliament as a 'permanent democratic forum'. Wales has not been democratically governed at any point in its recorded history; the measure of devolved government that now exists is the closest we have ever come to it.

The circumstances surrounding Glyndŵr's revolt may shed some light on the relationship between Wales and its monarchs, not only because of the way in which Owain himself approached the problem of kingship, but because of the revolt's context in English history. It was immediately preceded by the overthrow of King Richard II, to whom the Welsh apparently felt a degree of loyalty, and the usurpation of the throne by King Henry IV, for whom they seem to have had altogether different feelings.

When, in 1399, Richard of Bordeaux, son of the Black Prince and himself formerly prince of Wales, was toppled from the throne he had held since he was a boy of 10, there was outrage in the principality. This king was personally known to many of his people; he had been seen in Wales on several occasions. His father, though not universally popular when prince of Wales, had led Welshmen into battle with considerable success, thus contributing significantly to their self-esteem and helping to reinstil feelings of pride in their nationality. The Black Prince had been the first to give his men a uniform, on the grounds that English soldiers might not otherwise recognize their Welsh-speaking comrades as part of the same army.

Owain Glyndŵr was not the first rebel to have come to the fore since Edward I completed his conquest of Wales. The best-known of his predecessors, Owain Lawgoch (*c*.1330–78), who actually *was* descended from the royal house of Gwynedd, had made some progress towards international recognition, but his attempts to reinvade Wales had been dogged by misfortunes such as bad weather and lack of finance. It may be that, had he not met such a premature end, the English royal family would have had an earlier reminder of their unpopularity and would have had to rethink their attitude to Wales a little sooner.

It is worth looking more closely at the career of Owain Lawgoch in order to discover the differences, if any, between him and Glyndŵr. Was there anything in his approach that caused him to fail where Glyndŵr succeeded? There are plenty of possibilities. For example, was Glyndŵr a more charismatic man, a better leader, a more gifted politician than Owain Lawgoch? These are questions that are difficult to answer from mere written records, which are all we have. Glyndŵr had been born and brought up in Wales, whereas Owain Lawgoch had been born in England and spent much of his life in France. Did the failure of the native population to identify with their would-be prince have something to do with it, or was it simply bad luck? Did the conduct of the contemporary rulers of England really make any difference one way or the other?

Unlike Owain Glyndŵr, Owain Lawgoch was directly descended from Llywelyn Fawr, through Llywelyn's illegitimate son Gruffydd (d.1244). Gruffydd had four sons: the youngest, Rhodri (*c*.1230–*c*.1315), kept out of the dynastic struggle and became to all intents and purposes an English gentleman. Rhodri was the grandfather of Owain Lawgoch. Despite having been brought up as a member of the Welsh royal family, Rhodri apparently had no great love for his native land, and his grandson was born in Surrey, where Rhodri had acquired the manor of Tatsfield. Owain ap Thomas ap Rhodri trained as a soldier in France, where he effectively worked as a mercenary until, in 1369, King Edward III decided to take his English estates from him.

To us, this seems hardly surprising; Owain was, after all, fighting for the other side. This was the point at which Owain's military successes (he had made something of a name for himself by his bold and skilful leadership) led to his being recognized by King Charles V as a potential weapon against the English. Owain led a band of mercenaries that apparently included many Welshmen. His lieutenant, Ieuan Wyn, claimed descent from Ednyfed Fychan (d.1246), the right-hand man of Llywelyn Fawr. Almost as soon as he had made his decision to fight the English to get his lands back, Owain was provided with a fleet that set sail from Harfleur, bound for Wales. It was soon forced to turn back by bad weather. After faithful service on behalf of the French, he made a further attempt in 1372. This time Owain Lawgoch's men got as far as Guernsey before being recalled by Charles V to fight elsewhere. It was not until 1377 that rumours of a third attempt began to circulate.

All the factors previously mentioned played a part in the story; but the activities of the English monarchs also had some effect. Owain Lawgoch lived during the reigns of Edward III and Richard II. The English crown was not universally loved in Wales, and the regime was not much less oppressive than it had been under Edward I, in the early post-conquest period. Although secure enough on the throne of England, Edward III was concerned about the problem of law and order, especially on the borders of his kingdom. During the rebellion against his father, a severe outlaw problem had developed in the Severn valley, and in 1347 royal representatives were sent to Gloucester to deal with it.

In 1369, when the French wars once again became a going concern, Edward decreed that men from Shrewsbury should remain at home. He saw danger beyond the Welsh border, and wanted a force left behind to deal with it. He was aware of the presence of Welsh mercenaries fighting for France against him. His son, the prince of Wales known to posterity as the Black Prince, was already in failing health and by 1370 was no longer able to carry on the military campaigns that had been his chief pastime and pleasure up until then. Edward III made a point of increasing the strength of his Welsh castles in preparation for a potential invasion.

Owain Lawgoch died an ignominious death, assassinated by a Scotsman, one John Lamb, who was in the pay of the English. This was in July 1378, nine years after Owain had first staked his claim on the principality of Wales. He was probably already in his fifties, and would have had to overcome many obstacles to have made much more progress in pursuit of his claim. Edward III had died in the previous year, and there was a new, young king, Richard II, whose birth had taken place on the Feast of Epiphany and had been auspiciously attended by three kings. The period of Richard's minority was, admittedly, a danger period, but it was also a period of guarded optimism for the Welsh, who saw reason to hope that the boy might turn out less harsh a man than his father and grandfather.

When Henry III gave the royal possessions in Wales to his son, the future Edward I, in 1254, he was creating what the Normans called an 'appanage', a portion of land earmarked as the property of the heir, to be administered by him independently of his father. When, in 1397, Richard II created a new 'principality' of Chester to add to the existing one (which, since he had no children, he did not need to give up to his eldest son), his motives were more complex. He was building a personal empire, a region from which he could be sure of drawing support.

Just to be on the safe side, Richard gave parcels of Welsh land to his chief supporters, men like Robert de Vere, earl of Oxford, to whom he also gave the unprecedented title 'Duke of Ireland'. De Vere was in such great favour that he was allowed to divorce his wife, the king's first cousin Philippa de Coucy, in order to marry a lady-in-waiting who had arrived in England in the train of the young queen, Anne of Bohemia. Other royal favourites included William le Scrope, Thomas le Despenser and Richard's half-brother, John Holland, duke of Exeter, who became constable of Conwy Castle in 1394. As the reign of Edward II had already shown, building up such a close circle of favourites was almost to invite discontent among those who were not part of it.

Rarely has a king of England had such a mixed press as Richard II. As a boy, he had startled the whole country with his precocious courage and coolness in the face of the Peasants' Revolt. In August 1387, aged 20, Richard made his first personal visit to Wales. Although he had looked to the principality for support, he was not making a social call. Tired of having to do as he was told by his most powerful nobles, he had gone to the principality, in the company of Robert de Vere, to rally support against an anticipated rebellion. De Vere went on to lose to Richard's errant cousin, Henry Bolingbroke, at the Battle of Radcot Bridge, and fled into exile.

Having temporarily overcome the obstacles to his exercise of power, Richard continued to frequent the Welsh borders. In 1394, he was at Chester, preparing for a military campaign in Ireland. He held a parliament at Shrewsbury in 1398 (by which time he had acquired a personal bodyguard of two thousand Cheshire archers). The cross of Canterbury was brought to Shrewsbury for the occasion, and it was on this that the members of the parliament took their oath.

Henry Bolingbroke was banished from the kingdom in the same year, along with his enemy the duke of Norfolk. Richard's intention in removing the two men from his realm was to keep the peace; but he had not forgotten Bolingbroke's role in the unrest of 1387. When Bolingbroke's father and Richard's loyal uncle, John of Gaunt, died in 1399, Richard still bore enough of a grudge to decide that Bolingbroke should not receive his rightful inheritance. His Welsh estates were shared among the king's favourites.

In July 1398, Richard's heir presumptive, Roger Mortimer, 3rd earl of March, head of the powerful Marcher family, was killed in battle against the Irish clans. His body was brought home to Wigmore for burial.

Richard's response to the tragedy was to launch yet another military campaign against the Irish. He sailed from Milford Haven; no sooner was his back turned than Henry Bolingbroke returned from exile and made a bold attempt to seize the throne. As soon as the news reached the king, his key commander, the earl of Salisbury, was sent back to the mainland to assess the situation on his behalf, with instructions to raise the Welsh against Bolingbroke.

Salisbury arrived in Conway with every reason for confidence. A contemporary French chronicler makes the extravagant claim that 40,000 men were mustered in Richard's name, within the space of a few days. The strength of Richard's cause in Wales seems to have waned when the people became aware that their monarch was still in Ireland, awaiting developments. Rumours began to circulate that he was already dead. By the time Richard did arrive, a fortnight later, and landed at the port of Milford Haven from which he had originally set sail, Salisbury had been forced to retreat within the walls of Conway. (The author of the chronicle commented on the fine slate roofs of the houses in the town.)

Richard made his way quickly to Conway with a few companions, including the bishop of St David's, one Guy Mone. Following his meeting with Salisbury at Conway, he found himself deserted by the constable of Conway Castle. That there was still considerable enmity between the English and the Welsh is shown by the fact that the constable and his men were robbed of all the treasure, horses and the like that they were taking with them (their intention being to go over to Bolingbroke). According to the chronicle, they were left with nothing but the clothes they stood up in. The Welsh presented this deed as one of loyalty to King Richard. Nevertheless, they allowed the king to proceed practically undefended to his fateful encounter with Bolingbroke.

The duke of Exeter, one of Richard's Holland half-brothers, proposed that the king send him as an ambassador to Bolingbroke, to try to make some kind of peace. Richard himself, in the meantime, moved on to Beaumaris Castle on Anglesey, and from there to Caernarfon, which he decided was more easily defensible. Be that as it may, Caernarfon Castle had gone downhill since the days of Edward I, and was no longer a comfortable residence for a king. There was no furniture, and Richard was forced to sleep on a bed of straw. It was not long before he returned to Conway. Exeter made his representations to Bolingbroke, and was promptly made a prisoner in Chester Castle.

Moving on into Wales, Bolingbroke took the small castle of Holt and the larger one of Rhuddlan with virtually no opposition. Arriving at Conway, he persuaded Richard to leave the comparative safety of the castle under the pretence of negotiations. The king was taken to Flint by the earl of Northumberland, Henry Percy (1341–1408), who had been a loyal supporter of Richard's until alienated by the promotion of his greatest enemy. Northumberland's importance for Welsh history did not end when he escorted Richard to Flint; he would have a pivotal role to play in the struggle for supremacy between Henry IV and the Welsh rebels.

Henry IV, however, had many failings as a king. Aggressive and resentful towards his admittedly temperamental cousin, Henry met his first opposition from Richard II's former supporters. Chief amongst these were the earl of Salisbury and the duke of Exeter, the latter having been demoted to mere earl of Huntingdon as a result of his earlier championship of Richard. In January 1400, the Epiphany Rising took place, culminating in a scuffle at Cirencester as the two earls and their comrades headed for Wales, where they expected to find support for their cause. Salisbury and his nephew, the earl of Kent, were summarily executed. Exeter and the other ringleaders soon met the same fate. The rising convinced Henry IV of the need to place Richard II beyond help, and the deposed king, a prisoner in Pontefract Castle, was dead by February, possibly starved to death.

Owain Glyndŵr had, at one time or another, served in the armies of both Richard II and Henry Bolingbroke. He owed loyalty to both, and to neither; yet it is doubtful he would ever have rebelled against the English crown had it not been for Richard's overthrow. Although Richard's body had been put on public display, so as to scotch any rumours of his survival, there were plenty of doubters among the English population as well as the Welsh. Owain himself must have been in little doubt that Richard was dead, but he turned the doubts to his own advantage. He was not, after all, interested in ruling England, only in administering an independent Wales.

Owain Glyndŵr's use of a golden dragon as his battle standard drew on traditional emblems. Arthur 'Pendragon' was one of many who had used it before him. Hence it was associated with the concept of the 'mab darogan', the 'son of prophecy', for whom the Welsh were waiting. Another Welsh leader who had used the emblem previously had been Owain Lawgoch, who is depicted with a similar banner in medieval manuscripts. Owain Glyndŵr's personal bard and prophet, Crach Ffinnant, was one of those who advised him on when and how to trade on his popular image.

If Crach Ffinnant was Owain's Alastair Campbell, then Gruffydd Yonge (c.1370–c.1435) was his Peter Mandelson. Yonge was a leading churchman who had been in favour with Richard II. Through his relationship with Owain he made himself a bishop, a status to which he clung even after

Owain's disappearance. Had his prince's plans for Wales ever come to fruition, he could have expected to become an archbishop.

The best stroke of luck Owain had in the whole of his rebellion was the capture of Edmund Mortimer at the Battle of Bryn Glas (also known as Pilleth) in 1402. Mortimer's pedigree was royal through and through. Not only was he a direct descendant of Edward III through his mother, he was also descended from Welsh royalty through his father, whose line sprang from an ancestor's marriage to Llywelyn Fawr's daughter Gwladus. Edmund's elder brother, Roger, would have been next in line for the English throne after King Richard II, had Roger not died in 1398, leaving an infant son to inherit both his earldom of March and his place in the succession.

The Mortimers were disgruntled at having lost their status as heirs when Henry Bolingbroke usurped the throne, but they continued to serve the crown. If only Henry's loyalty to them had been equal, he would have ransomed Edmund Mortimer as was the custom with noblemen taken by the enemy in battle. This he failed to do, presumably because he feared Mortimer as a possible rival.

Although it was Edmund Mortimer's nephew and namesake, the little earl of March, who should have been next in line to the throne, the prospect of another boy king was not relished by the English. In Wales, though it is true that boys not yet in their teens had been known to take an active part in warfare, child kings and princes were virtually unknown, and Edmund Mortimer the uncle therefore began to be seen as a possible alternative to the House of Lancaster. If Henry IV could recognize this, so could Owain Glyndŵr, and he took advantage of the young man's presence in his home to forge an alliance that could only be advantageous to the Welsh cause. Edmund Mortimer married Owain's daughter Catrin with apparent willingness, and they soon had sons with the potential to inherit both the Welsh and English thrones.

When Glyndŵr's French reinforcements arrived in Wales in 1405, they were taken to Caerleon to view the remains of the Roman amphitheatre. In this place, many believed, lay the origins of the legend of King Arthur's Round Table. This, they thought, had been the site of his royal court. The association of Caerleon with Arthur seems to have begun some time in the Middle Ages, and was known to the French as well as to the Welsh. 'King Arthur – that fearless knight and courteous lord, removed to Wales, and lodged at Caerleon-on-Usk, since the Picts and Scots did much mischief in the land.' So wrote the twelfth-century poet Marie de France, in one of her *lais*. Gerald of Wales had fostered the myth, describing how the Romans had sent their ambassadors to Arthur's court at Caerleon. (Gerald, like most contemporary writers, never bothered to check his facts, since these were unimportant in the context of medieval literature. His only concern was to write things that people wanted to read.)

Whether or not Owain Glyndŵr believed the stories, it suited him to encourage his supporters to see him as King Arthur's natural heir. To this end, he laid out his plans for a utopian Wales in his 'Pennal policy' of 1406: it would have two universities and its own archbishop His plans were never realized, but, for a while, in his stronghold of Harlech, Wales's answer to Camelot must have looked a distinct possibility.

It was sensible of Owain to put his ten-year forward plan in writing. Other rebels had short-term gains in view, but Owain quickly realized that the initial momentum of his revolt would be lost unless he had something more tangible to offer his followers. He did not simply mean to overthrow Henry IV and drive him out of Wales; he intended to take Henry's place as Wales's king. To Owain, that meant actually running the country.

Less sensible, with hindsight, was Owain's decision to proceed with the Tripartite Indenture, even after the death of his English ally, 'Harry Hotspur', at the Battle of Shrewsbury in 1403. Hotspur's father, the earl of Northumberland, was elderly, older than Owain himself, but he had a thirst for revenge. He and his son had served Henry IV well until his disregard for their ability led them to negotiate with Owain. The loss of his son must have made Northumberland even more determined to overthrow the usurper. The plan to divide the whole of England and Wales into three parts (Owain was to rule Wales, Mortimer the southern half of England and Northumberland the northern half) was an almost inevitable consequence of the alliance, but it was not thought through. The English might not have loved Henry Bolingbroke, but they did not want to replace him with *two* petty kings. Wales had been a collection of small principalities from Roman times right up to the conquest of Edward I, whereas England had had more than four hundred years to get used to the idea of being a single kingdom under a single undisputed ruler. The idea of splitting it into two nations, ruled by nonentities like Mortimer and Northumberland, held little appeal.

The status of king is normally inherited. It follows that one of the essentials for any king is an heir. This is something to which Owain seems to have paid little attention. We know that he had at least two sons. He also had a son-in-law who was of royal descent and, in the eyes of the Welsh, heir to the English throne. To whom did he plan to hand over the reins of power when his own career was at an end?

Although we do not know Owain's exact date of birth, it is certain that he was a mature man by the time he raised his standard at Glyndyfrdwy in September 1400. His age has been estimated at 50, an age at which most men are beginning to think seriously about the future, about retirement, about their descendants and their legacy. By the time Owain disappeared from the records, he must have been (by the standards of his day) an old man.

Perhaps the presence of Edmund Mortimer in Owain's household had made him careless about the future; or perhaps he did not want to think about what might happen if Mortimer became king of England and one of his own sons prince of Wales. Either way, he seems not to have protected his family adequately. His wife and daughters were abducted from Harlech Castle when it was stormed by Henry of Monmouth, and were taken as prisoners to London, where they eventually died of unknown causes. Edmund Mortimer had died at Harlech; history does not record exactly when or how, but plague has been theorized as an alternative to a violent death. Without him, Owain's cause crumbled. One of his sons survived him, as we know from the fact that Henry V issued a pardon to Maredudd ab Owain in 1421. By this time Maredudd seems to have lost interest in reviving the cause of an independent Wales, and it is possible to attribute this fact, at least in part, to Henry V's success in dealing with the principality in which he had spent so much of his youth.

As in the case of Owain Lawgoch, so much depended on the contemporary political climate in England. Henry V was a popular ruler for the short period of his reign, his personal CV strengthened by the miraculous victory at Agincourt. His only child was a baby when crowned King Henry VI, and this might have been a good time for a further rebellion in Wales, had it not been for two factors. One was the fact that so many Welshmen were now in the pay of the English crown; Henry V had drawn them to him by his personal charisma, and had given them the self-esteem on which they thrived by allowing them to play such a pivotal role in his victories.

The other factor was the lack of a leader in Wales. Owain's son clearly did not wish to be involved, and there was no one else with a claim to Welsh royal blood who was not already reconciled to the idea of Wales being annexed to England. There may even have been a third factor. Henry V's widow, the French princess Catherine of Valois, having been rejected by the English court the moment her husband died, soon found solace in the arms of a Welsh gentleman, Owain Tudor (d.1461), by whom she had several sons. Two of these boys, Edmund and Jasper, were recognized and ennobled by their half-brother King Henry VI, creating another good reason for Welshmen to become loyal to the House of Lancaster.

# The Wars of the Roses

⤳

Rebellion did not altogether cease simply because Owain Glyndŵr had disappeared from the scene. The cause of Welsh independence became subsumed by the greater political struggle that began when it became clear that the young Henry VI was not going to be the strong and warlike king his father had been. The Welsh had not altogether forgotten how the House of Lancaster had usurped the throne from the House of York, and there were men still living who had fought under Glyndŵr.

Richard Plantagenet, duke of York (1411–60), returned from Ireland in 1450, shortly after the loss of Calais to the French, to find himself more popular than the king. York had inherited the estates of the Mortimer earls of March (his mother Anne (1390–1411) having been the sister of the last earl), and he could consequently rely on a strong following in the Welsh border country. York landed at Beaumaris and marched on London, his aim being to seize control of the government from the advisers the king had favoured. Having got the better of his rivals, he returned temporarily to his castle at Ludlow, gathering more support for a further confrontation with the king.

When Henry VI suffered some kind of mental breakdown, York was appointed 'Protector of the Realm', and for a few years he more or less ruled England and Wales. When Henry recovered, however, the in-fighting between two of England's most powerful families, the Percy family (led by the latest earl of Northumberland, the son of Harry Hotspur) and the Neville family, reached its peak. Richard Plantagenet found himself on the opposite side from the king as the disagreement degenerated into a feud between the Houses of York and Lancaster. The Battle of St Alban's in 1455 marked the beginning of a civil war that would continue, on and off, for the next fifteen years.

Henry VI's queen, Margaret of Anjou, now took up an aggressive stance on behalf of her husband. Her main concern seems to have been for her son, the infant prince of Wales, who she feared would be supplanted by the duke of York and his descendants. The Battle of Blore Heath, in 1459, brought the struggle right to the doorstep of Wales. The population of Cheshire was split down the middle, and in Wales loyalties were also divided. This pattern continued. Following the death of the duke of York in the following year at the Battle of Wakefield, his son, later King Edward IV, became the Yorkist heir. The battle that clinched victory for Edward was that of Mortimer's Cross, which took place in Herefordshire, only a short distance from Wigmore, ancestral home of the Mortimers.

The Yorkist army in that battle included Gruffydd ap Nicolas, a Montgomeryshire man who had been governor of Cilgerran Castle under King Henry VI but had switched sides. His decision was the result of King Henry's own foolishness in allowing his half-brother, Jasper Tudor (c.1431–95), to take the governorship of Cilgerran for himself. It was Jasper who led the opposing Lancastrian army, along with his father, the notorious Owain Tudor, secret husband of Henry V's former queen. Following the defeat of the Tudors, Jasper escaped, but Owain was executed. Shortly before his death the old man is said to have commented that 'the head which used to lie in Queen Catherine's lap will now lie in the executioner's basket'.

One chronicler, speaking of the Yorkist successes, records that 'Such favour had the commons of Wales to the Duke and his affinity that they could suffer no wrong nor evil words to be spoken of him or his friends.' In spite of this, it was to Wales that Queen Margaret fled, with her little son, Edward of Westminster, following the decisive Battle of Towton in 1461. The boy had been invested as prince of Wales in 1454, but when Henry VI's successor, the Yorkist Edward IV, produced a legitimate heir in 1470, the latter was quickly invested with the title. The result was that once again there were two princes of Wales in existence, each with an equal claim on the title. This time, however, both were English-born and had little knowledge of the principality.

King Edward IV set out to correct this. He had grown up in the border country, and had been earl of March since 1460, when his father, the duke of York, was killed. Edward had drawn much of his own support from the Welsh Marches, and had gathered an army of eight thousand men to fight on his behalf at Mortimer's Cross. He was now intent on building up a similar following that his son could rely on when he became king himself, as seemed likely to happen in due course.

Not long before the birth of the new prince of Wales, Edward IV was still facing opposition in Wales. Harlech Castle was in the hands of Dafydd ab Einion, a die-hard Lancastrian supporter, until May 1469, when William Herbert, earl of Pembroke (and the grandson of Dafydd Gam, another die-hard Lancastrian), succeeded in coming to terms with the opposition after an unsuccessful siege. This was not the end of Edward's problems. He had fallen out with his long-standing mentor, the earl of Warwick. Warwick, 'the Kingmaker', having visited Margaret of Anjou in

France and married off his younger daughter to the Lancastrian prince of Wales, returned to England intent on replacing Henry VI on the throne. This he succeeded in doing, but it was only a temporary setback for Edward IV. By the time Margaret of Anjou and her son were back in the kingdom, her husband was once more in captivity and the earl of Warwick was dead. At the Battle of Tewkesbury in May 1471, Edward of Westminster, son of Henry VI, became the only prince of Wales ever to die in battle. The Lancastrian army had relied for its salvation on Jasper Tudor, and he had been unable to reach them in time.

Jasper's earldom of Pembroke had been confiscated when Edward IV took the throne but temporarily restored to him by Warwick's rebellion. There, on his return, he found his 14-year-old nephew, Henry Tudor, in the care of the dowager countess of Pembroke, the former Anne Devereux, herself descended from a Norman Marcher family. Henry's father, Edmund Tudor, had died in 1456 before the boy was born. Now young Henry was briefly introduced at court before being forced to take refuge in Brittany by the unexpected return of Edward IV from exile.

Henry Tudor was a Welshman destined for greatness, but not until the House of York had at least attempted a political reconciliation with Wales. Edward IV's young son was publicly invested as prince of Wales as soon as Henry VI and his son had been eliminated. While still a toddler, the new prince, Edward by name, was packed off to Ludlow to ensure that 'by the authority of his presence the wild Welshmen and evil disposed persons should refrain from their accustomed murthers and outrages'. A tall order for such a small person.

The prince relied on his uncle, Anthony, Earl Rivers, to administer justice in the principality. Rivers was often in Wales, but the prince could not venture out without an escort, and there is no official record of his having crossed the present-day border. It was not the most normal upbringing for a small boy, but that is an occupational hazard of being heir to the throne. His mother and father visited him often. Even in Shropshire and the neighbouring English counties, he would have come across many speakers of the Welsh language; and there was no shortage of Welshmen paying visits to Ludlow to plead their various causes and pay allegiance to the child, who, they anticipated, would remember them when he became king.

What no one anticipated was that the day of Edward V's accession would come so soon. Edward IV was barely 40 years old when his life of fighting and womanizing took its toll. According to the bard Lewys Glyn Cothi, the prince of Wales was actually in his principality with his uncle on that day in 1483 when the news arrived of the king's death. They were reported to be suppressing some local unrest that had broken out; we know no other details of this. On their return to Ludlow, they found a message awaiting them from the queen. The party set off as soon as possible for London, where a coronation was planned. One of the new king's companions was the soldier and diplomat Sir Thomas Vaughan.

To the Welsh people, as to the English, the death of King Edward IV brought uncertainty, but there must have seemed no immediate cause for concern. The prince was 12 years old, not far short of the age at which previous kings such as Edward III had taken the reins of government; and he had already been given a good grounding in the craft of kingship. Moreover, should any misfortune befall the new young king, the succession was assured in the shape of his younger brother Richard. Both boys had some acquaintance with Wales.

What happened next is history, and well-known history. Edward IV had several younger brothers, only one of whom had survived the king. He was Richard, duke of Gloucester, and he hated the queen and her relatives, who wielded immense influence and had been gradually edging him out of the royal favour over a long period. Despite this, it was to the duke of Gloucester that Edward IV had entrusted the protection of the realm in the event of his death.

Within three months of Edward IV's death, Richard had succeeded in eliminating all his rivals. He had the two princes declared illegitimate on the grounds of the supposed illegality of Edward IV's marriage to his queen, and had himself crowned king. The fate of the princes is unknown, but there is enough circumstantial evidence to make historians believe that Richard had them murdered.

Sir Thomas Vaughan was only one of many casualties of Richard III's rise to power, and was executed not long after the young king's maternal uncles. Vaughan, from Monmouth, had some history of double-dealing. He had served King Henry VI and had a close association with Jasper Tudor, but had been loyal to Edward IV since the latter ransomed him from French pirates in 1462. It is perhaps not surprising that Richard did not trust him.

Another man Richard would have been well advised not to trust was Thomas Stanley, who was now married to Margaret Beaufort (1443–1509), the mother of the young Henry Tudor. Margaret Beaufort was now at the forefront of the anti-Richard campaign, and sent her personal physician, a Welshman named Lewis, to negotiate with Elizabeth Woodville, the widowed queen of Edward IV, who had gone into sanctuary at Westminster Abbey for the second time in her life. Messengers were sent to Brittany, where Henry Tudor waited with his uncle Jasper for the right moment to invade. The dean of Bangor, Richard Kyffin, is said to have sailed across in an open fishing-boat to reassure the Tudors of their north Wales support.

The Wars of the Roses had not yet reached their conclusion. Towards the end of 1483, Richard was obliged to fight off a rebellion led by his former ally Henry Stafford, duke of Buckingham, who is thought to have been motivated by Richard's failure to give him the de Bohun estates which he had coveted for many years. While Richard was thus preoccupied, the Tudors planned an invasion attempt. Sir Rhys ap Thomas (1449–1525), another Welsh royalist, was preparing to support the king against Buckingham when he received an approach from Margaret Beaufort's Dr Lewis, who persuaded him to switch sides. Sir Rhys, described by the pro-Yorkist bard Guto'r Glyn as 'the greatest hero of his day', would have been an exceptionally useful ally.

Sir Rhys met Buckingham at Trecastle near Brecon, where the duke was amassing support from his Welsh estates; but at the same time Richard, suspicious of the Welsh knight, insisted on his giving up his 5-year-old son as a hostage to assure his loyalty to the crown. Buckingham raised his rebellion at Brecon Castle in October, but his progress towards London was impeded by floods at Weobley in Herefordshire. Deserted by many of his Welsh supporters at this point, and seriously outnumbered by the king's approaching army, he found himself a fugitive in the border country. He was soon captured by the authorities in Shropshire. Buckingham was swiftly executed, and the Tudors were forced to abandon their invasion attempt by adverse weather conditions.

Sir Rhys ap Thomas had managed to avoid committing himself to either party until the rebellion was over, but he now became a ringleader of the Tudor cause. Other Welshmen involved in the conspiracy included the bishop of St David's, Thomas Langton, and the abbot of Talley. It was not until August 1485 that the Tudor invasion plans finally came to fruition and these men finally obtained their most fervent wish: a Welshman on the throne of England, and a permanent end to the Wars of the Roses.

Richard III, in the early part of his reign, had gone on a 'progress' through his kingdom which took him as far as Gloucester and Tewkesbury, but not into Wales. This might have made it difficult for him to convince the Welsh of his interest in them. He had, however, inherited the title of lord of Glamorgan through his wife, Anne Neville (1456–85), who had in turn inherited it from her father, the earl of Warwick.

The Church of Holy Cross in Cowbridge was awarded a charter by the king, of which the 500th anniversary was celebrated in 1985. The parishioners are evidently not too troubled by the idea that their patron might have murdered his royal nephews. He was the king, and his apparent interest in lowly Cowbridge is still remembered with gratitude by today's residents. When Prince Charles visited the church in 2004 to celebrate the anniversary of the original town charter, all royal connections were brought to his attention by his entourage. The enduring connection between church and state was nowhere more clearly seen than in the special service he attended, in the company of local dignitaries. It is a connection that has been assumed by kings and princes since the earliest days of the Christian religion; but it was only with the Tudor dynasty that it acquired the closeness it has today.

# Welsh Royalists

## MARCHER LORDSHIPS

It is tempting to think of Wales as a politically radical country with a tradition of republicanism. Nothing could be further from the truth. English kings have drawn some of their most loyal support from the principality. The Welsh were prepared to follow their native princes to the end. When these were replaced by alternative rulers, many subjects transferred their allegiance without a qualm. Edward II, Edward III, the Black Prince, Richard II, Henry V, Edward IV and Edward V were all indebted to their faithful Welsh supporters. The role played by Welsh archers at the battles of Crécy, Poitiers and Agincourt is well attested.

Even before the Norman conquest of Wales was complete, there was no shortage of Welshmen prepared to follow English kings into battle. One of the reasons for Henry II's willingness to make peace with Rhys ap Gruffydd was that he was preoccupied with his Irish campaign and needed free access to the south Wales ports in order to ship his troops across the sea to Wexford. In 1169, a force set out under the leadership of Richard de Clare, second earl of Pembroke, known to history as 'Strongbow'. De Clare's incentive for the campaign was the same as that of any Marcher lord. He hoped to acquire additional estates and wealth, as Henry had given him the title 'Lord of Leinster' in anticipation of his success in adding to Henry's kingdom.

'Strongbow' acquired support, not only from his Welsh vassals, but from other Welshmen who joined the army en route. It was dangerous, but for a poor man it was a living, not to mention the opportunity for plunder. The skill of archery was already greatly valued, and it was a skill common in parts of Wales. Many of the Welshmen who had followed the English army to Ireland remained there, hence the existence of surnames like Walsh and Wogan in the Irish Republic today, indicating Welsh descent which generally originates from this period.

A notable Welsh rebel of the post-conquest years was Llywelyn Bren (d.1318), who led a rising in Glamorgan during the reign of King Edward II. Although the king commanded some loyalty in Wales, his favourites did not, and it was the younger Despenser who went back on his

word and had Llywelyn Bren and his men executed after he had volun-
tarily surrendered. There will have been few tears shed in Wales when,
eight years later, Despenser suffered exactly the same fate, being hung,
drawn and quartered at Hereford, while Roger Mortimer (who had been
responsible for the capture of Llywelyn Bren and respected the
Welshman's courage) looked on with satisfaction.

Llywelyn Bren was not a born rebel. All accounts agree that he was a
man of culture and considerable property, goaded into his revolt by the
unfair treatment he had received at the hands of Norman officialdom,
following the death of Gilbert de Clare, the young earl of Gloucester, at the
Battle of Bannockburn. Llywelyn had been on good terms with de Clare,
but the failure of a direct appeal to King Edward II caused him to become
disillusioned with the English crown, and he had little difficulty in raising
a following among his disgruntled compatriots. His unpleasant fate was a
reminder of Norman military might, and there was no further rebellion of
any significance in Wales until 1400.

Not all Welshmen supported the revolt of Owain Glyndŵr either. Dafydd
Gam (c.1380–1415) was a conspicuous exception, a man with impeccable
Welsh credentials whose family had nevertheless supported their Norman
overlords from the earliest days. Dafydd Gam opposed Glyndŵr with all his
might, and eventually died fighting for Henry V at Agincourt alongside
many of his compatriots. Nor was he Glyndŵr's only Welsh opponent. In
1402, Jenkin Howard, constable of Dinefwr Castle, wrote to the 'receiver' of
Brecon to warn him of Glyndŵr's activities. It was only natural that those
who had prospered under the Normans should have lacked sympathy with
those who sought to dismantle the existing political structure.

On the other hand, Glyndŵr's rebellion was not without its English
supporters. The Percy and Mortimer families were foremost among these.
The Mortimers, of course, were by this time almost as Welsh by blood as
they were English. Constance of York (d.1416), a daughter of Edmund of
Langley, attempted to arrange the escape of Edmund Mortimer's young
nephew, the earl of March, who had been King Richard II's designated
heir. Her motives clearly had more to do with a hatred of Henry IV than
with any love for the Welsh. As for Henry Percy, earl of Northumberland,
and his son Harry Hotspur, their league with Glyndŵr was also born of
discontent with the current king.

## THE TUDOR CONQUEST

Under the Tudors, Welsh support for the English monarchy naturally
became stronger. It is understandable that Henry Tudor, born in

Pembroke, should have chosen to return via that route in order to collect local support before marching north to meet the usurper Richard III in battle. When Henry began his invasion attempt, however, it was with an army of Frenchmen. Only after his arrival in Wales did he begin to amass a force of his compatriots, chief among them being Sir Rhys ap Thomas. The wily Welsh knight, having previously sworn an oath of fealty to the incumbent king, Richard III, to the effect that anyone who invaded Wales would have to pass over his belly, lay down on his back under a bridge so that Henry could ride over him.

Henry landed at Dale, a small port in Pembrokeshire close to present-day Milford Haven. It was a spot that had been identified by the authorities as a potential landing-place, but the invasion force was large enough to see off any opposition quickly; not that there was much of that. That Henry foresaw some support from his fellow countrymen is shown not only by the decision to land in his native county, but by the fact that he had arranged to meet his supporters in Shrewsbury, enabling him to march through most of south and mid-Wales en route. Many Tudor adherents had already gathered in Pembrokeshire, including local gentry such as Sir Thomas Perrott of Haroldston and Sir John Wogan of Wilston Castle. Henry himself headed for Shrewsbury via Cardiganshire, and Sir Rhys via Carmarthenshire, both collecting followers as they progressed.

The result of Henry's accession was that Wales, the scene of many rebellions and revolts in the previous 200 years, suddenly became the source of the king's strongest support. Welshmen flocked around him, and many received his favour. After Henry Tudor, it was less difficult for a Welshman to show allegiance to the English crown. Although Wales, as a political entity, had no independent existence, there was a perception that the very fact of the new king being Welsh made the crown as Welsh as it was English. Consequently, there was no reason to rebel.

Clifford S. L. Davies, writing on 'The Tudor Delusion' in the *Times Literary Supplement* (11 June 2008), noted that the Tudors seldom made reference to their surname during their time on the English throne. Nothing new here; the same might be said of the Windsors. The corollary, Dr Davies suggested, was that there was no such thing as a Tudor dynasty or 'Tudor England'. He pointed out that Elizabeth of York, like her husband, was descended from Cadwaladr (d.682), a king of Gwynedd, and therefore had an equal right to call herself Welsh. All this may be true, but it does not alter the fact that the Welsh saw Henry VII as one of their own, regardless of whether they called him Henry Tudor or Henry, earl of Richmond. They would remember the origins of his family long after the English had forgotten them.

Henry recognized the need to keep the Welsh on his side. He appointed commissioners to look into his pedigree and trace his descent from Ednyfed Fychan. According to the findings of commissioners, his ultimate ancestor was Beli Mawr, a legendary figure of the Roman period. More significant was his descent from Cadwaladr, 'the hundredth King of Britain and the last' (if Geoffrey of Monmouth is to be believed). The popular fashion for all things 'British' that surfaced during the reign of Elizabeth I was partly a way of contrasting the solid descent of her family from the ancient rulers of Britain with the fancy French origins of her chief rival, Mary, queen of Scots. It was useful to the propagandists that the Tudors could prove themselves a home-grown royal family, especially bearing in mind that Henry VII himself had been a quarter French and had spent much of his youth abroad.

In fact, Henry Tudor did not claim the throne by right of his royal blood. He would have been on shaky ground, since his mother's family, the Beauforts, had been banned from acceding to the throne at the same time they were legitimized by King Richard II. Henry's claim was based on the right of conquest and the right of possession, just as that of his half-great-uncle, King Henry IV, had been. Strangely, one never reads of the 'Tudor conquest of England' in history books, but that is exactly what it was. The reality is that Henry's claim on the English throne was about as good as that of William the Conqueror.

In 1495, Henry actually visited Wales, calling at Hawarden Castle in Flintshire, where his mother lived with her third husband, Thomas Stanley, now earl of Derby. Stanley's brother William, who had been a staunch supporter of the Tudors at the time of the invasion and had been instrumental in Henry's success at the Battle of Bosworth, had been found guilty of treason and executed. His crime was to have supported a pretender, Perkin Warbeck, who claimed to be Prince Richard, the younger brother of the late King Edward V. (Warbeck's attempted invasions capitalized on the Cornish uprising of 1497, but he had no substantial support and was eventually captured and executed in 1499.) Henry had wasted no time in appropriating Holt Castle, Stanley's home in what is now a suburb of Wrexham, but he made the effort to visit his stepfather in order to avoid any danger of the elder brother going the way of the younger.

In his concern to retain the loyalty of his Welsh followers, Henry went further. He took a leaf out of Edward IV's book, sending his son and heir, Arthur Tudor, to administer Wales on his behalf from Ludlow Castle. It was a well-intentioned move, and the early years of Arthur's stay were useful, helping the heir to the throne to learn the ropes. Arthur was not, however, a robust youth. When, in 1501, the prince of Wales married the

Spanish princess, Catherine of Aragon, everyone must have been hopeful that a child would soon follow and the succession would be assured. Although, in 1498, the Spanish ambassador wrote that Henry's hold on the throne was undisputed and 'his government is strong in all respects', he also wrote that Henry was 'not a great man' and was 'disliked' by his subjects. By contrast, it was said of Arthur that the people 'love the prince as much as themselves'. A child for Arthur and Catherine would set the seal on the future of the Tudor dynasty. Although both bride and groom were only 15 at the time of their marriage, such things were not unheard of. Henry Tudor's own mother, Margaret Beaufort, had been only 13 when she gave birth to her son.

Unfortunately for Henry Tudor and for the principality, Arthur and Catherine both fell ill at Ludlow after a few months of marriage. Catherine recovered, but Arthur died, leaving his younger brother Henry to take on the mantle of heir to the throne. Henry was quickly invested as prince of Wales, and was even betrothed to Arthur's widow, but he never took up residence at Ludlow.

During the reigns of Henry VII and his children, there were numerous uprisings – Lincoln's rebellion in 1487, the Pilgrimage of Grace in 1536, Sir Thomas Wyatt's rebellion in 1554, and of course Essex's in 1601. None of these found any groundswell of support in Wales, and this was partly because the royal family in London was now so strongly associated with the principality. Henry VIII and Elizabeth I certainly capitalized on their Welsh blood, even though neither of them ventured further west than Bristol.

Sir Griffith Rice, the son of Rhys ap Thomas (who had already anglicized the spelling of his name), was present at the investiture of Henry Tudor's son, Arthur, and was made a Knight of the Bath. In 1520, still in royal service, Sir Griffith accompanied Arthur's younger brother, King Henry VIII, to the Field of the Cloth of Gold in France. Sir Griffith's son, Rice Griffith, succeeded to the family estates in 1522, but was executed in 1531. His treason was to have taken an additional name – Rice ap Griffith fitz Urien. The name honoured Urien Rheged, a sixth-century British ruler and supposed follower of King Arthur. The family claimed descent from Urien, and that alone would have been enough to put Rice Griffith in the king's bad books; but there was more. Rice's mother was the former Katherine St John of Bletso, making him a distant cousin of the king. There was no room for family feeling in Henry VIII's make-up. He saw every family tie as a potential threat, and several innocent relations who had been spared by his father (notably the 67-year-old Margaret, countess of Salisbury) met their deaths under the axe during his reign.

The Acts of Union of 1536 and 1543 finally put an end to the power of the Marcher lords to do as they liked in Wales and the borders. Henry VIII wanted no opposition to his rule in any part of his kingdom. 'Justice is not administered there in such form as in other places of this realm', noted his new statute, and this was a good argument for the creation of a new legal and administrative structure, bringing the principality into line with the rest of the country. Amongst other things, the traditional Welsh system of inheritance, whereby property was shared equally among the sons of the deceased, was abolished.

It would be wrong to assume that Henry VIII was being dictatorial when he imposed the Acts of Union on his kingdom. He did in fact receive a petition from Wales, stating that its subjects 'do crave to be received and adopted into the same laws and privileges which your other subjects enjoy'. The petition referred back to the services performed by the Welsh for earlier kings, including their loyalty to Edward II, Edward III and Richard II. Despite the admitted existence of 'refractory persons', they pointed out that the majority of Welshmen had been contented with the rule of Henry V and had made up for their subsequent support of the House of York by their devotion to Henry Tudor. The authors of the petition even went so far as to ask to be allowed to use English more extensively: 'it shall not hinder us to study English, were it but to learn how we might better serve and obey your Highness, to whose laws we most humbly desire again to be adopted'.

On reading such words, Henry VIII could hardly refuse to grant the petitioners the privileges they requested. Whether the authors of the petition were genuine in their request, or whether they were merely attempting to curry favour with the king, by asking him to act as they knew he planned to do anyway, is a cause for speculation. Whether they really wanted it or not, they got it.

In 1535, the king, through his 'vicar-general' Thomas Cromwell, sent agents into Wales to carry out the 'Valor Ecclesiasticus', a survey whose purpose was to assess the value of the property that would pass to the crown when the monasteries were dissolved. Evidence was gathered of ill-doing in some of the abbeys (alleged counterfeiting in Strata Florida, for example) so as to help justify the dissolution. In 1536 all the smaller monasteries were closed down; the only ones remaining open at this point were Whitland, Strata Florida and Neath Abbey, and these did not survive much longer.

It would be wrong to imagine that the Welsh were up in arms over the closure of the monasteries. The Pilgrimage of Grace was a movement that began and remained in the north of England, and there was no major public protest in Wales. There were, however, individual complaints. Ellis

Price, commissary-general of the diocese of St Asaph, wrote to Thomas Cromwell to warn him of the difficulty he had encountered in getting the local people to give up an image of 'Derfel Gadarn', a saint associated with Arthurian legend. *Hall's Chronicle*, published in 1542, records how the image was removed from its shrine and taken to Smithfield to be burned. There may have been more to this than met the eye. Derfel Gadarn was more than a religious icon; he was a symbol of Welsh independence, a rallying-cry for Owain Glyndŵr's rebels. This was a good opportunity to eradicate a folk memory that might have led the Welsh once more into revolt.

Individual Welshmen of the upper classes profited by the dissolution, acquiring church property and in some cases making their homes in the former abbeys; Ewenny Priory is a good example. Margam Abbey passed into the hands of Sir Rice Mansel (d.1559), whose descendants owned the estate until 1941. Sir Rice, being Sheriff of Glamorgan and one of Henry's Commissioners of the Peace, was in a good position to take advantage of the opportunity. Others were not so lucky. For the ordinary people of Wales, the change meant new landlords; for the wealthy, it meant a redistribution of power within the principality.

Henry VIII did not choose to visit Wales in person. He had lost a brother at Ludlow who got too close to the principality. The king did, however, recognize his father's heritage by giving Henry Tudor's old title, earl of Richmond, to his own illegitimate son. Henry Fitzroy, born in 1519, was the child of a mistress, Elizabeth Blount. In 1535, the boy, who had been married off to the daughter of the duke of Norfolk, travelled to Holt in Flintshire, to visit one of the properties given him by his doting father.

The following year Henry VIII, desperate for an heir, succeeded in persuading Parliament to allow him to dispose of the succession in his will. This gave him the option of recognizing Henry Fitzroy, illegitimate as he was, as the heir to the throne; the option of giving him the new title 'king of Ireland' was also considered. Had Henry been able to legitimize his son without legal impediment, a divorce from Catherine of Aragon might never have been needed. Unfortunately for the king, and significantly for the realm, Henry Fitzroy died in that same year, probably from tuberculosis.

Fortunately for the king, when he was in the middle of his reorganization of the kingdom, a legitimate son, Edward, was born to his third queen, Jane Seymour. One of the ideas that was considered, and rejected, before deciding on the form the new government of Wales might take, was a separate principality, to be ruled by the young prince. This would have been a kind of formalization of the existing role of the prince of Wales, an extension of the powers of the heir to the English throne.

Any sensible administrator would have foreseen problems with this proposal. Henry VIII himself had been faced with so many obstacles in his quest to father even one legitimate male heir (and a sickly one at that) that it would have been asking for trouble, even without the worrying examples of Edward Plantagenet and Arthur Tudor to look back on. Moreover, a boy of the prince's age could hardly have been expected to stamp his authority on the government of a territory the size of Wales without parental intervention. What Wales needed was a strong administration to replace the free-for-all it had undergone at the hands of royal favourites and powerful landowners. The future Edward VI was never even created prince of Wales.

By 1543, Wales had acquired five new counties (giving it thirteen in total) and the right to send representatives to the English parliament. The Marcher lordships, by contrast, had lost almost all their power. Although order was in part restored by these measures, there was still unrest in Wales over the way that justice was administered. Rowland Lee (d.1543), titular bishop of Coventry and Lichfield, had been appointed president of the Council of Wales and the Marches in 1534 by Thomas Cromwell, Henry VIII's chancellor. Lee was described by a near-contemporary, William Gerard, as 'stout of nature, ready of wit, rough in speech', and most importantly, 'not affable to any of the Welshry'. Lee's reputation as the scourge of criminals and outlaws was such that the poet Myrddin ap Dafydd produced a popular ballad, urging bandits to join together and fight for freedom. 'Mae clogyn Rowland Lee i'w foddhad yn goch o'n gwaedu ni,' says the verse: 'The cloak of Rowland Lee, to his relish, is red with our blood.'

As a result of the same redistribution of power, the county of Monmouthshire was in the Welsh Marches. Although technically and geographically in Wales, it was grouped with the neighbouring English counties for the purposes of administering justice. Its inhabitants proceeded to develop an identity crisis from which they are only just recovering.

Protestantism flourished in Wales under Henry VIII's immediate successor, his teenage son Edward VI, and in 1547, the first year of Edward's reign, the publication of portions of scripture in the Welsh language was begun by Sir John Price (c.1502–55) and William Salesbury (d.c.1584). There was a setback for this process when the king died, aged only 15, in 1553, and his sister Mary came to the throne. The Protestant martyrs of this period get a lot of publicity, but there were only three of

1. Plaque commemorating Gwenllian, last of the royal line of Gwynedd.
*Photo © Princess Gwenllian Society*

2. St Winifred, the Welsh princess whose relics were removed from Holywell to
Shrewsbury Abbey, where a window now commemorates her.
*Photo © Deborah Fisher*

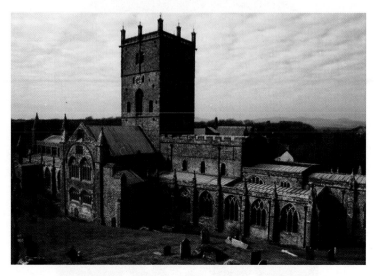

3. St David's Cathedral, one of the oldest places of Christian worship in Britain, represented a challenge for William the Conqueror.
*Photo © Rhys Jones, LRPS*

4. The tomb of Roger de Montgomery, Norman earl of Shrewsbury, a key figure in the English Crown's campaign to dominate Wales.
*Photo © Deborah Fisher*

5. Caernarfon Castle, where Queen Eleanor gave birth
to the first 'English' prince of Wales in 1284.
*Photo © Rhys Jones, LRPS*

6. Conway Castle, a lavish royal residence for King Edward I but a less comfortable resting-place for his great-great-grandson King Richard II.
*Photo © Rhys Jones, LRPS*

7. The town of Monmouth still takes pride in the achievements of its favourite son, King Henry V of England.
*Photo © Rhys Jones, LRPS*

8. Tredegar House, looking much as it did when the Morgan
family entertained King Charles I here in 1645.
*Photo © Deborah Fisher*

9. Demonstrating that mass-produced royal souvenirs are not a modern
phenomenon, this jug commemorates the silver wedding of the
prince and princess of Wales in 1888.
*Photo © Deborah Fisher*

10. Raglan Castle, home of the marquess of Worcester, was deliberately ruined by Parliament's forces in revenge for its owner's support of the Royalist cause during the English Civil War.
*Photo © Rhys Jones, LRPS*

11.  Prince Albert 'the Good' looks down on the citizens of Tenby.
*Photo © Deborah Fisher*

12.  A bicycle decorated with flowers to mark the jubilee.
*Photo © Powysland Museum, Welshpool*

All days of Glory, Joy and Happiness.
Shakespeare.

QUEEN ALEXANDRA

KING EDWARD VII

PRINCE EDWARD OF YORK

PRINCESS OF WALES

PRINCE OF WALES

THREE GENERATIONS.

Raphael Tuck & Sons "Empire" Postcard Series 609.
Designed in England Chromographed in Bavaria.

13. Three generations of princes of Wales are depicted
on this postcard from the early 1900s.

them in Wales. Robert Ferrar, bishop of St David's, was one. The English-born Ferrar lost his position for being married, and was burned at the stake as a heretic. It was customary for such executions to take place in the town where the victim was best known; consequently Ferrar was tried, convicted and (having refused to recant) died at Carmarthen in 1555.

Mary had been brought up a Catholic, and detested the new religious structure which had been responsible both for the downfall of her mother, Catherine of Aragon, and for her own past misfortunes. In 1526, as the heir to the throne, Mary herself had been sent to Ludlow Castle to preside over the Council of Wales and the Marches. Shortly afterwards, her father made the decision to divorce her mother, and her position became untenable. She was demoted to the rank of 'Lady' and banished from court while her younger sister, Elizabeth, became flavour of the month. (Elizabeth never made it to Ludlow; her mother, Anne Boleyn, was disgraced and executed before Elizabeth herself was 3 years old.)

Following the accession of Elizabeth I, a petition was made to Parliament by William Salesbury for the whole Bible to be translated into Welsh. The order, passed in 1563, took account of the fact that 'the most and greatest number of all her Majesty's most loving and obedient subjects inhabiting within her Highness dominion and country of Wales, being no small part of this realm', did not understand English. Elizabeth, who inclined towards Protestantism on the grounds that Spain and the pope were ready to replace her with her Catholic cousin, Mary Stuart, at the earliest opportunity, no doubt hoped that the availability of Bibles in the language of the people would consolidate her position as ruler and head of the Church of England.

Elizabeth was by no means a friend to all Protestants, however. Wales's most famous martyr, John Penry, was put to death in 1593 on a charge of treason, having spent much of his life on the run from the religious author-ities. His only real offence was to have made a rough draft of a petition to the queen, in words that were considered seditious by his arch-enemy, Archbishop Whitgift.

In general, Elizabeth inherited her grandfather's interest in the princi-pality, and gathered about her Welsh acolytes such as the redoubtable Blanche Parry (d.1590), Keeper of Her Majesty's Jewels. Blanche's relative, Eleanor Bull, was the keeper of the Deptford tavern where Christopher Marlowe met his end in the same year as John Penry. Marlowe's contem-porary, William Shakespeare, acknowledged Elizabeth's ethnic background with references to Wales, suggesting that his audiences were familiar with the concept of Welshness. The character of Fluellen in Shakespeare's *Henry V* is said to have been partly based on Roger Williams

(1540–95), the famous Welsh soldier of fortune who followed Dutch Protestant leader William the Silent and apprehended William's assassin.

Like Blanche Parry, Sir Richard Bulkeley (d.1621) spent much of his life at court. He inherited the position of MP for Anglesey from his father, another Sir Richard Bulkeley. Sir Richard, being a member of the Council of Wales and the Marches, was involved in the commission appointed in 1568 by the queen, attempting to control the activities of 'minstrels, rhymers and bards' within the principality. Wales already had the 'Statute of Gruffydd ap Cynan', prepared for an eisteddfod at Caerwys in Flintshire fifty years earlier, a document cataloguing the regulations by which the practitioners of this craft were meant to abide. Now a second 'congress of bards and musicians' was summoned to meet at Caerwys, and Simwnt Fychan was appointed 'pencerdd', giving him some seniority within the profession.

Taking over the position of head of the family in 1572, the second Sir Richard Bulkeley gradually found himself in opposition to the powerful Robert Dudley, earl of Leicester (the man whom many suspected of being Queen Elizabeth's lover). Leicester's sister, Mary, was married to Sir Henry Sidney (1529–86). When Sidney was appointed president of the Council of Wales and the Marches in 1560, the family duly moved into Ludlow Castle, where their children were born, including a daughter, Mary (1561–1621), who became one of the first notable women writers in the English language.

In 1563, thanks partly to his closeness to the Sidneys and partly to his friendship with the queen, Leicester was created Baron Denbigh and given Denbigh Castle along with the lordships of Denbigh, Bromfield and Yale. Almost immediately he trebled the rents payable by his tenants. Popular feeling over his treatment of them was so great that, when he enclosed common land, the locals tore down the fences. Leicester's arrogant conduct continued.

When the well-loved Sir Henry Sidney died in 1586, the presidency of the council passed to his son-in-law, Mary's husband, Henry Herbert, earl of Pembroke (1534–1601). The importance of marriage alliances in maintaining the prosperity of noble families had not altogether declined, and Mary's younger brother, Robert Sidney, had married Barbara Gamage (1563–1621), Wales's greatest non-titled heiress, in 1584. It was probably in that same year that Leicester obtained the position of Custos Rotulorum ('keeper of the rolls') of Anglesey, which had previously been held by Sir Richard Bulkeley.

Shortly after Henry Sidney's death came the discovery of the Babington Plot, in which a group of Roman Catholic conspirators, led by Sir Anthony Babington, entered into secret correspondence with Mary, queen of Scots, with a view to putting her on the English throne in place of Elizabeth. They had no idea they were being set up by Francis Walsingham, Elizabeth's spymaster. The result was their capture, and the eventual execution of the queen of Scots. Two Welshmen were involved on the fringes of the plot. Thomas Salusbury had been a servant of the earl of Leicester, but, while in London, he had converted to Catholicism. Edward Jones, of Plas Cadwgan in Denbighshire, was the son of Elizabeth's master of the wardrobe and another hanger-on of Leicester. Witnesses stated that the two men had been heard plotting a popular uprising in Denbighshire, in Mary's favour. This was ironic in view of the damage to public relations in the county that had been done by Leicester himself.

Both young men were captured and executed. A third Welshman whose complicity in the plot was proven was Thomas Morgan of Llantarnam (1546–1606). Morgan was a staunch Catholic, and had corresponded with the queen of Scots from the Scottish embassy in Paris. He had in fact helped to recruit Babington to the cause. When the plot was discovered, Morgan was placed in the Bastille prison by the French authorities, and remained in confinement for several years. He never returned to the British Isles.

All three of the Welsh conspirators were from landed families, Thomas Salusbury being the son of the notorious Katheryn of Berain (1534–91). Katheryn is sometimes referred to as 'Katherine Tudor', giving the false impression that she was a close relative of the royal family. One of her grandfathers, Sir Roland de Velville (1474–1535), is thought to have been the only recorded illegitimate offspring of Henry Tudor; but the truth of this is unknown. Katheryn's four marriages and six children resulted in a genealogy that won her the nickname of 'mam Cymru', 'mother of Wales'. Her four husbands, Sir John Salusbury, Richard Clough, Maurice Wynn and Edward Thelwall, were all wealthy men with substantial estates in Wales.

Other powerful families with estates in the Welsh Marches included the Devereux clan, the most notable of whom, Robert Devereux, was largely brought up in Wales. In 1576, at the age of 9, he inherited his father's title of earl of Essex, and shortly afterwards his mother became the secret second wife of none other than Robert Dudley, earl of Leicester. When the secret came out, the queen was livid, and banished Leicester from court. After a few years in the political wilderness, however, the earl was recalled, and brought with him his handsome stepson, who almost immediately became Queen Elizabeth's new favourite. Like so many others, Essex allowed power to go to his head. The half-hearted rebellion of 1601, which resulted in Essex being executed for treason, was one of the last major events of the reign of Queen Elizabeth I.

## THE STUARTS

The Welsh were already coming to London in droves to make their fortune (as they had been for the previous two centuries at least), and they did not stop coming when the Stuarts, and later the Hanoverians, became the ruling dynasty. The eighteenth-century Morris brothers of Anglesey were the best known of these London Welshmen, but there had been a Welsh presence in the capital city long before that. One Henry le Waleys was lord mayor of London three times during the late thirteenth century; the name clearly indicates Welsh origins.

In 1606, the Union Flag, now better known as the Union Jack, came into use as the standard of the united kingdoms of England and Scotland. There was no room for a Welsh symbol on the flag, nor any thought of one, since Wales was already considered to have merged with England. It was not a question of Wales being a subsidiary 'country' that had been conquered by England. Wales was *part* of England. Whilst retaining its own customs, language and other characteristics that we associate with nationhood, it was no more a nation than Cornwall or Kent.

King James VI of Scotland had become king of England (and hence of Wales) in 1603. By virtue of being a Scot, James aroused some interest among the Welsh. Genealogies were quickly drawn up, revealing his descent from the Welsh royal line and making it clear to any doubters that he was also a direct descendant of Henry Tudor. 'Brenin Siams', wrote the bard Richard Phillips, 'Cymro yw hwn' ('King James ... is a Welshman').

Nevertheless, it was his elder son, Henry, who first drew the new king's attention to the principality's significance. In the year of James's accession, John Davies of Hereford (d.1618) published his *Microcosmos*, which included not only dedicatory verses to the new monarch and his queen, but a poetic epistle from 'Cambria' to the boy Davies assumed would be given the title of prince of Wales.

Henry's personal acquaintance with the principality was limited to official correspondence, such as a letter of 1607 from Thomas Stephens, mentioning 'the principality of Wales, a great country and dominion, containing twelve shires, which the kings of this realm have used to confer upon the princes their eldest sons'. Almost as soon as he heard this news, he virtually insisted on being invested with the title (and naturally also the revenues that went with it), and the ceremony took place in 1610.

The prince's death, two years later, was a bitter blow to the Stuart dynasty, even though he had a younger brother, Charles, to assume the title in his place. John Davies of Hereford was one of those who bemoaned Henry's loss most loudly. His poem *The Muses-teares for the Losse of Their*

*Hope* was published in 1613. It was not an original idea; the very title was borrowed from earlier works by Edmund Spenser and others, and it was traditional to offer panegyric verses for any royal (or indeed any patron) who died. Davies's description of Henry as 'heroick and ne'er too much praised' does, however, genuinely reflect the high regard in which Henry was held, and the disappointment felt by many Welshmen who had hoped for so much from the promising youth. Henry's accession to the throne had been anticipated by the whole of Protestant Europe, and his younger brother already looked like a poor substitute.

Charles was invested as prince of Wales in 1616, and the occasion was celebrated with the performance of a masque specially written for the occasion by the poet laureate, the great Ben Jonson. King James made no secret of the fact that he found the masque boring, and Jonson followed up, early in 1618, with a more entertaining work entitled *For the Honour of Wales*. In this 'anti-masque', several hapless stereotypes with names like Jenkin and Evan discuss how they can improve on the earlier work. They end by stressing their allegiance to the crown, asking the prince and his father to 'pardon what is past, and remember the Cymru has always been fruitful of loyal hearts to your Majesty; a very garden and seed-plot of honest minds and men'.

In the meantime, in 1617, James had made his only visit to his native Scotland since his accession to the English throne. On his way back to London, he took the opportunity to tour other parts of the realm, accepting hospitality from noble families (and sometimes coming close to bankrupting them). In August he visited the city of Chester, where he was rapturously received. Even at this date, there is evidence that the Welsh recognized the new Scots royal family as having a close ethnic relationship with the people of the principality.

When Charles I succeeded his father, he could, like any former prince of Wales, rely on a certain amount of support from the principality. Wales had become primarily royalist, mainly because of its geographical and political profile. There were no large towns as there were in England, and consequently there was little in the way of trade and industry. Most people made their living off the land, poor as it was, and they did as they were told by the small number of powerful individuals who owned that land. These families, who had gained their property through royal favour, continued to support the king.

The Welsh, though not as deeply embroiled in the Civil War as were the English and the Scots, did see some action on home soil. Even when there was no actual fighting going on, many were obliged to choose sides. One such was John Jones, Maesygarnedd, who supported Parliament throughout the struggle. He was described by one contemporary as 'the most hated man in North Wales' for his perceived disloyalty to the crown. Jones married Oliver Cromwell's sister in 1656, but his closeness to the seat of power did him no good at all when the monarchy was restored, for he was a 'regicide', having signed the death warrant of King Charles I in 1649. For this treason he was brutally executed, along with several others, in 1660. His fellow countryman and regicide, Thomas Wogan (c.1620–c.1666), escaped with his life but was obliged to flee abroad.

In John Jones's case, his religious beliefs clearly had much to do with his attitude towards the king. Whereas James I had brought up his sons to believe they were appointed by God and had a 'divine right' to rule, Jones belonged to the 'Fifth Monarchist' sect, who looked forward to Christ's second coming and the establishment of his rule over the earth. Naturally, the idea that a mere mortal should be regarded as having the final say in how they lived their lives was anathema to them.

Other Welshmen were equally fervent in their support of Charles I, and their preference did not necessarily depend on their religion or politics. Many simply felt that it was morally wrong to take up arms against their king. Almost the moment the war broke out, Charles received unsolicited petitions of support from all over the principality. We need not read too much into this; those who support the winner can expect to be rewarded after the victory. It must, at that time, have appeared unlikely that Parliament would be able to defeat the king in a single battle, let alone a war. The groundswell of support was nevertheless present in Wales, and it was on this that Charles gradually fell back as he found his position in the rest of the country more and more difficult.

During the early months of the war, Wales was not completely isolated from its reality. Individuals declared for one side or the other, and castles changed hands. In Bangor, Colonel Thomas Mytton (1608–56) plundered the house of Sir Gerard Eyton. Parliament's fleet took the king's ammunition store on the Mawddach estuary. Major Vaughan of Pant-glas was killed in the taking of Hopton Castle near Ludlow. Cardigan town was taken by the 'men of Pembrokeshire'. In September 1643, Vavasor Powell, the notorious Nonconformist preacher, led a march of eighty men to Machynlleth.

In January 1644, the conflict escalated. At Nantwich in Cheshire, a town occupied by Parliament's forces, the great general Thomas Fairfax managed to break a six-week siege by his Royalist opponents. This caused some panic in Chester, a city loyal to the king, and defensive works were quickly thrown up. The authorities received assistance from their neighbours in north Wales, who, as can be inferred from the comments about

John Jones, were Royalist almost to a man. The king himself arrived in Chester in September, and was received with ceremony and enthusiasm, despite the fact that his armies were, by this stage, very much up against it.

Parliament had soon taken Hawarden and Wrexham. In the meantime, Prince Maurice (brother of the dashing Prince Rupert of the Rhine) headed for Chirk Castle in an attempt to draw the opposition away from Chester. The castle's owner, Sir Thomas Myddelton (1586–1666), was a committed Protestant who had declared for Parliament and was the brother-in-law of the rampaging Colonel Mytton. However, the Royalists had held the castle since early in 1643, having taken it whilst Myddelton was busy trying to cut off their supply routes in north Wales. In September 1644 the first battle took place on Welsh soil, at Montgomery. The result was another defeat for the king, but his forces continued to hold Chirk and Denbigh.

One of Henry VII's original Welsh supporters had been Sir John Morgan (d.1492), 'Y Marchog Tew' ('the fat knight'), the ancestor of the family of Morgan of Tredegar Park in Monmouthshire. The Morgans remained loyal to the crown, and William Morgan held the appointment of recorder of Brecon and king's attorney for south Wales throughout the Civil War. On 16 July 1645, the Morgans entertained King Charles I to dinner and an overnight stay at their Tredegar estate. On 25 July, he was with another branch of the family at Rhiwperra. Despite the recent catastrophic defeat of the king's army at the Battle of Naseby, the Morgans and other landed families of south Wales remained loyal to their monarch.

Colonel Edward Prichard (d.1655) found himself in a quandary. Having served the king faithfully in the early years of the war, he saw which way the tide was turning, and by 1645 his loyalty was wavering. Charles, hearing a rumour that Prichard was thinking of going over to the opposition, visited him at his home, the manor of Llancaiach Fawr, on 5 August (a fortnight after visiting the Morgans at Tredegar Park), in an attempt to persuade him otherwise. Almost as soon as the king had departed, Prichard defected to the cause of Parliament, and in the following year he defended Cardiff Castle against the Royalist forces, his former comrades. Prichard's home is now a museum of living history.

One of the most important of Charles I's supporters in the latter part of the war was Henry Somerset, marquess of Worcester (d.1646), who held the appointment of lord lieutenant of Glamorgan and Monmouthshire. The marquess entertained the king lavishly at Raglan Castle in September 1645. Less than a year later, however, General Thomas Fairfax besieged the castle and the marquess of Worcester was forced to surrender. Parliament's army took its revenge by 'slighting' the castle, making it uninhabitable. It remains a ruin, but, thanks to Cadw, visitors can get an idea of the grandeur of the castle in the days when it played host to a king and his retinue.

Later in September 1645 the king was again in Wales, taking refuge at Denbigh Castle. Its governor, Colonel William Salusbury (d.1660), was known to his contemporaries as 'Hen hosannau gleision' ('Old Blue Stockings'). Salusbury and Sir Thomas Myddelton had been friends prior to the outbreak of the war, and an exchange of polite correspondence between them during 1643 has survived. Myddelton requests of his former friend that he should 'please to submit yourself to the power and obedience of *the King and* Parliament, lay down your arms, and deliver up that castle'.

Salusbury (who was of course a member of that same prominent family that had produced a Babington Plotter in the previous century) responded that 'I desire not to live longer than I approve myself true to my King and country, a true lover of the Protestant religion, and that yield cheerful and hearty obedience to my King and Parliament.' Thus Welshmen on both sides considered themselves loyal subjects of the king as well as respectful towards Parliament, and stressed their adherence to the Protestant religion. Sir William did not give up the castle until October 1646, long after the king's visit. (Even then, he did so only with the king's written approval.)

The king stayed at Denbigh for one night only, marching on the following day to Chester, where he witnessed at first hand the events of the Battle of Rowton Heath. It was a decisive victory for Parliament, no doubt made more painful for the Royalists by the fact that the victorious commander, Michael Jones (d.1649), had fought for the king in Ireland, where his father, Lewis Jones, was bishop of Killaloe. Jones had gone over to Parliament in 1643 because he disapproved of the truce the king had signed with the Irish 'Confederates'. He was evidently one of those whose first loyalty was to his religious beliefs.

It might be supposed that the king's imprisonment, following the near-destruction of his armies, meant that the Welsh could return to a more peaceful way of life. However, once the king was in the power of Parliament, dissent broke out between those who had fought against him because they opposed his rule and those who had done so as a temporary measure, hoping that the monarch would be able to settle his differences with Parliament as soon as the war was over. Sir Thomas Myddelton, who had made such a contribution to the Parliamentary cause, now began to see that the outcome would not be as he had hoped. His brother-in-law, Thomas Mytton, had done well out of the war, and quickly put down the last-minute rebellion of the doughty Royalist, Sir John Owen of Clenennau (1600–66).

Myddelton, Mytton and John Jones Maesygarnedd were also among five commissioners appointed by Parliament to deal with the island of Anglesey, which continued to hold out for the king as late as July 1648. Led by well-known names such as Bulkeley and Wynne, the people of the island issued a declaration to the effect that they continued to be loyal subjects with the country's best interests at heart, and it was those who opposed them who were the traitors.

The Civil War was already virtually over when, in April of that same year, 1648, a group of Cromwell's most trusted officers, disgusted at the treatment meted out by Parliament to its unpaid and disaffected troops, went over to the Royalists. Chief among these was Rowland Laugharne (d.1676), a prominent Parliamentary leader up to this point. Laugharne, with his fellow commanders John Poyer and Rice Powel, led their army eastwards from Pembrokeshire to meet the Cromwellians near Cardiff. On this occasion, Colonel Edward Prichard was among those who remained loyal to Parliament and defeated the rebels at the Battle of St Fagan's, the most significant Civil War action to take place in Wales.

A postscript to the events of 1648 in south Wales was the discovery, in 1996, of the Tregwynt 'hoard', a treasure unearthed at Tregwynt in Pembrokeshire. The hoard of gold and silver coins is believed to have been buried around that time, though by whom is not known. It is assumed that it was the property of Royalists, who feared the outcome of Laugharne's rebellion and were preparing to be besieged or driven from their home. Why they never returned to claim their cash will remain a mystery.

Sir John Owen of Clenennau, breaking the terms of his previous surrender, had hoped to join up with Laugharne's forces, but his campaign was ineffectual. Condemned to death for treason, Sir John was eventually allowed to retire to his much-reduced estates. Sir Thomas Myddelton was responsible for the sequestration of Owen's estates, and dealt leniently with him. Myddelton also opposed the trial of King Charles I, and was soon completely out of favour with Cromwell and excluded from Parliament.

The former prince of Wales, Charles Stuart, had not given up his claim on the throne. He returned from his continental exile and, with the assistance of the Scots, marched south to confront Cromwell. The Battle of Worcester, in 1651, was a disaster for the prince, but his campaign demonstrated once again that any prince of Wales could be sure of some support from the principality. Following his defeat, he went from loyal house to house in the border area, staying overnight at Leominster, White Ladies Priory and Boscobel before making his escape to France via Bristol.

Cromwell himself, though ostensibly disdainful of the whole concept of royalty, was actually not immune to it. He ruled Britain with an iron rod, often disregarding the will of Parliament just as King Charles I had done. In 1657, having turned down the offer of a crown because 'I would not seek to set up that which Providence hath destroyed and laid in the dust', he nevertheless accepted additional powers as Lord Protector, and was invested with these in a coronation-like ceremony at Westminster Abbey. At the same time, Cromwell's pedigree was published, revealing him to be not only of Welsh descent but of Welsh royal blood, able to claim direct descent from Bleddyn ap Cynfyn (d.1075).

By 1651 Sir Thomas Myddelton, having for a time been forced to leave his home at Chirk, was openly supportive of the pro-Royalist movement. In 1659, after the death of Oliver Cromwell, he joined the Cheshire Rising begun by Sir George Booth, with a view to restoring the monarchy under King Charles II. The rising failed, and Parliament ordered that Chirk Castle be demolished. Happily, the order was never carried out. Within a year Charles II was on the throne, and Myddelton received £60,000 in compensation for his treatment. His son was created a baronet.

The Myddeltons were not the only Welshmen to profit from the restoration of the monarchy. In 1661, William Morgan of Tredegar had his posthumous reward for his loyalty to Charles I. William's granddaughter Blanche married her first cousin, another William Morgan, and the family's newly restored prosperity resulted in the building of a grand new mansion. Tredegar House can be visited by the public today, looking very much as it would have done in the late seventeenth century.

There were other ways of supporting the monarchy during the difficult time of Cromwell's rule. Leoline Jenkins (1625–85) (who anglicized his name from Llywelyn ap Jenkin to make himself more acceptable in English-speaking society) was not by nature a military man, and quickly withdrew from the fighting to set up a school at the home of his acquaintance, Sir John Aubrey (1626–97). Aubrey (best remembered as the author of *Brief Lives*) was of Welsh descent and owned a house at Llantrithyd in Glamorgan, where he gathered around himself other Welsh royalist refugees. These included Sir Francis Mansell (1579–1665), who in 1648 had been forced by Parliament to leave his position as principal of Jesus College, Oxford.

Leoline Jenkins acted as tutor to Aubrey's children, but was forced to leave after being charged with running a 'seminary of rebellion and sedition', and moved to Oxford where he attempted to resume his teaching. Once again forced out by the Parliamentary authorities, he spent some time in exile on the Continent. At the Restoration, Francis Mansell, who had already been allowed to return to his home in Oxford, was permitted to resume the principalship of Jesus College. When his health forced him to retire in 1661, his successor was Sir Leoline Jenkins, who continued to serve Charles II as a politician and a lawyer and died in the same year as his king.

Many of Charles II's loyal followers were created 'Knights of the Royal Oak' in recognition of services rendered during the most difficult time of his life, and these included many Welshmen. Names we might recognize among their number include those of William and Charles Salusbury, Sir Thomas Myddelton, Sir Roger Mostyn, Lewis Wogan and the heirs of Sir John Owen.

## JACOBITES

While an exile in Holland, Charles II had encountered the vivacious Lucy Walter, daughter of William Walter of Roch Castle in Pembrokeshire. When Roch was taken by Parliament in 1644, the family were driven out. Lucy ended up in The Hague, where she was introduced to the prince, by which time she had already been for a time the mistress of Algernon Sidney, a leading Parliamentarian. Rejecting Sidney and other lovers in favour of a potential future king, she gave birth in 1649 to a son whom Charles acknowledged as his own. The results of this liaison would be momentous.

Lucy Walter faded from the scene, dying in squalor in Paris before she was 30, but the child she had borne in Rotterdam remained in the care of his father and was duly created duke of Monmouth following the Restoration. When Charles's marriage to the Portuguese Catholic princess, Catherine of Braganza, proved childless, many began to feel that the best prospect for the country's future would be for him to be succeeded by almost anyone but his younger brother, James.

Charles II and James II had both been strongly influenced in religious matters by their mother, Henrietta Maria of France. Whereas Charles had been instilled with the importance of showing only his Protestant side in public, as a means of ensuring his hold on the realm, James had always been a devout Catholic and saw no reason to change. On the contrary, he would see his accession as an opportunity to improve the lot of Catholics throughout the land, at the expense of Protestants if necessary.

In 1682, before the hopes of the anti-Catholic faction had been completely dashed, the duke of Monmouth visited Chester. One of the dignitaries in the welcoming party was William Williams (1634–1700), who two years earlier had become the first Welshman to be appointed speaker of the House of Commons. Williams had been, and continued to be, an outspoken critic of the future James II. In 1684, however, he came into open conflict with a fellow Welshman, Wrexham-born George Jeffreys (1645–89), who took a legal action against him for having allowed the publication of the *Narrative* of Thomas Dangerfield, a pamphleteer and anti-Catholic agitator. As a result of his treatment by the courts, Williams came round to the king's side and by 1687 was James's solicitor general, involved in the prosecution of the 'Seven Bishops', a cause célèbre that proved a turning point in the king's political fortunes.

James II had not been king for four months when the duke of Monmouth, now a personable young man of 36, raised a rebellion against him. Monmouth claimed that his mother, Lucy Walter, had been secretly married to his acknowledged father, King Charles II, making him the legitimate heir to the throne. Some chose to believe it; but it was the wrong time for a rebellion, and Monmouth failed abysmally, losing first the Battle of Sedgemoor and, shortly afterwards, his life to the headsman's axe. Ironically, the savage putting-down of Monmouth's rebellion (including the activities of the 'Hanging Judge', George Jeffreys) added to James's growing unpopularity.

In 1686, James II made his only visit to Wales as king. He was desperate for an heir. With two daughters by his Protestant first wife, he needed to produce a son by his second wife, Mary of Modena, to ensure the Catholic succession. Mary had already given birth to five children, all of whom had died in infancy. The king's faith was such that he believed in the power of the holy waters of St Winifred's Well in Flintshire, and made a personal pilgrimage to Holywell. To the loyal subjects who attended him there, James gave out commemorative gold rings containing locks of his hair. Miraculously, the visit to Holywell seems to have had an effect. Five years after her last pregnancy, the queen conceived again, and her son, James Stuart, prince of Wales, was born alive and healthy in June 1688.

As the Civil War had clearly shown, the tradition of royalism might apply even when cultural factors such as religion militated against it. Wales is associated with Nonconformism, but Catholicism in the principality never died out. The duke of Monmouth's support had not come from Wales, and Wales still had its share of Jacobites (supporters of King James). Most notable among these was William Herbert, marquess of Powis (1626–96). It was Herbert who waited with a boat to rescue the queen, Mary of Modena, and her infant son, the prince of Wales, when King James II was forced off the throne in 1688 by his Protestant daughter, Mary, and his Dutch son-in-law, Prince William of Orange. Herbert took the royal mother and baby to France, where they received a warm welcome from King Louis XIV.

Sir William Williams, despite the honours he had received from King James II, was quick to revert to his old allegiances, and retained his position as solicitor general under the new joint monarchs. George Jeffreys, on the other hand, realizing that he had burned his boats by his support of James II, attempted to follow his king to the Continent, but was captured and died in prison the following year.

The 'Glorious Revolution', as the comparatively peaceful overthrow of James II came to be known, was not an event that proved particularly significant for the principality. William and Mary being childless, there was once again no prince of Wales, except for those who continued to regard James II as their rightful king (and there were many of these). This continued to be the case into the reign of Queen Mary's sister Anne, who came to the throne in 1702. Anne's many children had all died before her accession, and the question of who would succeed her gradually came to the fore as she aged.

Neither King William III, Queen Mary II nor Queen Anne ever stepped across the border into Wales, though William did pass through Chester on his way to Ireland, where the Jacobite resistance was strong and a military campaign had proved essential to maintain his hold on the kingdom. That William was not completely oblivious to the existence of the principality, however, is demonstrated by the case of the earl of Portland, William Bentinck, a politician of Dutch origin who was greatly favoured by the king. In 1696, Portland was granted the lordships of Denbigh, Bromfield and Yale, along with extensive estates in Wales. The Welsh gentry and MPs quickly made an official objection.

Robert Price (1653–1732), a justice of the Court of Common Pleas, spoke out against the grant in the House of Commons. His speech was later published under the title *Gloria Cambriae; or the Speech of a Bold Briton in Parliament against a Dutch Prince of Wales*. Price and his fellow countrymen argued that the lordships in question being part of the principality proper belonged to the crown and should not be lightly given away to any individual. The king took note of the complaint, and quickly withdrew the grant.

William had changed his mind, not in deference to the Welsh, but to the House of Commons. His lack of awareness of the history of the titles with which he had been so prodigal is hardly surprising. The emotive use of the word 'Briton', in the title of Price's speech, however, implies a certain xenophobia on the part of William's new subjects. They would rather have a Protestant king than a Catholic. Equally, however, they would rather have had a Briton than a Dutchman. William's wife Mary died in 1694, before the dispute arose, aged only 32. Throughout the seven and a half years that William survived her, he would be regarded with suspicion by the British, as an interloper whose presence was not entirely welcome. He was the king, but he enjoyed little affection from his subjects.

The decision to publish Price's speech only after William was dead must have had less to do with fear of the king's reaction than with a desire to please the new queen. Anne had not got on very well with her late brother-in-law. Those responsible for the publication wanted to show her how important it was to the people to be ruled by a woman who had been born in Britain and had spent most of her life there. True, she had a Danish husband; but Prince George, though a skilled military commander, had little to do with matters of state and knew better than to meddle in politics.

Jacobitism survived in Wales, particularly in landed families with a strong tradition of royalism, such as the Bulkeleys of Anglesey, who kept busts of the last Stuart prince of Wales and his two sons ('Bonnie Prince Charlie' and his brother Henry, duke of York) at their home in Baron Hill. William Herbert's daughter, Winifred (d.1749), showed the same indomitable spirit as her father, twenty-seven years after his exploits during the Glorious Revolution, when she rescued her husband, the earl of Nithsdale, from the Tower of London, where he had been incarcerated for joining the Jacobite Rebellion of 1715.

Welshmen were certainly involved in both the '15 and the '45, and it must be admitted that this had little to do with the fact that James Stuart had been prince of Wales or that his son, Bonnie Prince Charlie, claimed the same title. Nevertheless, there were elements in Welsh society who saw the Hanoverians as usurpers. Sir Watkin Williams Wynn (1692–1749), grandson of the Speaker Sir William Williams, was said to be the founder of the 'Circle of the White Rose', which met at his home on the great estate of Wynnstay. Unlike the many commoners who followed Prince Charlie to their deaths at Culloden, however, Sir Watkin got away scot free with his activities, and was never found guilty of any wrongdoing.

Others with Jacobite sympathies included Dr Alban Thomas, a graduate of Jesus College, Oxford. Dr Thomas abandoned his London practice suddenly in 1722. When he did return to the British Isles, it was to practise medicine discreetly in his native county of Cardiganshire, where the authorities were not likely to pursue him. Henry Lloyd of Merionethshire (d.1783) was a Welsh Catholic who went to France to seek a military commission and was an agent for the Jacobites during the 1745 rebellion, though he escaped with his life. David Thomas Morgan, a gentleman of

Glamorgan, was less fortunate. After his participation in the '45, he was taken prisoner, convicted of treason, and was hung, drawn and quartered on Kennington Common. It was a brutal penalty, allegedly invented by King Edward I for the last of his Welsh enemies, Dafydd ap Gruffydd (1238–83), and traditionally used on those who attempted to challenge the power of the English monarchy. By the eighteenth century, however, it was the government and not the king himself who demanded it; for the king no longer ruled Britain.

# The Path to Constitutional Monarchy

From this time onwards, the attitude of the English royal family towards Wales (and, to a lesser extent, Scotland) became less threatening and even more patronizing. Gone was the prospect of Welsh armed rebellion. The nearest the Welsh came to it was the industrial unrest that occurred in both north and south Wales as the coal and iron industries expanded rapidly; and the focus of discontent had now been transferred to the owners of those industries. As the monarch's power fell away or was taken away by Parliament, so other individuals became more powerful as a result of the wealth they had accumulated. Success in business transformed individuals into petty tyrants, who virtually had the power of life and death over those they employed. These were the natural successors of the Marcher lords.

William III and his immediate successors may not have been infected by it, but there was a growing awareness of 'Welshness' in England's capital city. One of the women Queen Anne could possibly have come across in the course of her routine was Mary Steele, née Scurlock, a Carmarthen heiress who arrived in London in about 1707. Her husband, Richard Steele, an Irish soldier and writer, obtained a position in the household of Prince George of Denmark. The marriage was a stormy one, and Mary (nicknamed 'Prue', short for 'Prudence', by her spendthrift husband) often retreated to Wales, leaving Steele to his own devices. Following her death, Sir Richard preserved his memories of her by retiring to Carmarthen, where he is buried.

With the death of Queen Anne, and the advent of the Hanoverian dynasty, things began to look even more promising for Wales. One prince who was undoubtedly aware of the existence of the principality, and who had a vested interest in so being, was Prince George Augustus, who became prince of Wales in 1714, shortly after the accession of his father, King George I. The new prince was a man of 31, married with children, and so Wales came to have not only its first titular prince for twenty-five years, but its first princess in over two hundred years.

Caroline of Ansbach, by a lucky chance, was not only attractive, talented and clever, but happened to have been born on the first of March.

This accident of birth gave her an immediate iconic status in the eyes of the London Welshmen, who were always on the lookout for ways of making their presence felt. Both Caroline and her husband quickly became conscious of the fact that there were certain revenues payable to the prince of Wales (with the approval of Parliament, of course). They set out to appear worthy of receiving this additional income, though their enthusiasm was not so great as to persuade them to visit the principality in person.

The new generation of royals considered it their duty to take an interest in Wales, especially if it was possible to do so without actually going there. Henry Stuart, who had persuaded his doting father to revive the title of prince of Wales for him in 1610, never actually visited his principality (or any other country apart from England and Scotland). His father, King James I and VI, did venture further afield in the course of his reign, but it was left to Henry's younger brother, Charles I, to form any real relationship with Wales and its people. As we have seen, this was a case of looking after royal interests. The farther reaches of the kingdom had ceased to be of much interest by the end of the seventeenth century, when any Welshman worth his salt would make his way to London if he wanted to be noticed.

The Hanoverians were starting from scratch, but their intentions were good. Although the new prince and princess of Wales had their work cut out to get used to the language and customs of England, let alone those of Wales and Scotland, the couple were prepared to do what was necessary to make themselves popular. Their eagerness to be liked increased when King George I ejected them from the royal palace after a very public quarrel.

Caroline commissioned the architect William Kent to build two cottages, or 'grottoes', in the grounds of Richmond Palace, one of which she named 'Merlin's Cave'. Her interest in Merlin, the legendary figure associated with King Arthur and to a lesser extent with Wales, was not new. It was said by some that Merlin had prophesied the coming of the Hanoverian dynasty. A life-sized wax dummy of the wizard stood inside the grotto, which Caroline's husband referred to as 'childish, silly stuff', according to the memoirs of her friend Lord Hervey.

Satirists, too, mocked the queen's hobby, but artists and writers had already begun to reflect this renewed interest in things Celtic. In 1724, Daniel Defoe began publication of the account of his *Tour through the Whole Island of Great Britain*. 'They value themselves much on their antiquity, the ancient race of their houses, families and the like, and above all, their ancient heroes', he noted, speaking of the Welsh and observing with disapproval that King Arthur had 'suffered much from legendary writers and tradition'. Defoe also notes the similarities between the Welsh and Cornish people and the affinity between their native languages.

Richard Morris of Anglesey (1703–79) first came to London in about 1721, and was visited there by his brother William, a botanist and anti-quary, in 1730, and by his youngest brother John, a sailor, in 1735. The eldest brother, poet and scholar Lewis Morris (1701–65), came to the capital in 1753 to seek legal assistance. Lewis was devoted to his homeland, and did not consider a permanent move. Richard, however, had been drawn there by his occupation as a book-keeper, and was disinclined to leave, perhaps because of his growing involvement in London Welsh society. Since the 1720s he had been a member of the Society of 'Ancient Britons', a charitable group formed at the time of the Hanoverian succession. In 1751 Richard founded the Cymmrodorion Society, with assistance from Lewis, who drew up a list of topics to be considered by its members.

Lewis was not by any means convinced that London was the place to be for a patriotic Welshman. Writing to his brother in 1761, he still appears sceptical about the value of the Cymmrodorion: 'being as yet but in its infancy, and begun by a Society of those Ancient Britains [sic] that reside in London, who are not to dictate to all Wales till their name is better established'. Lewis's primary concern was for the future of the Welsh language, and he deplored the practice of the charity schools in Wales of educating children through the medium of English: 'For this kind of education ... only enables them, like the Irish, to crowd over in droves to England, to the utter ruin of their place of nativity.' The Cymmrodorion were certainly convinced of the value of the language, and they had their own song, 'Nyni yw'r Hen Drigolion', which translates as 'we are the old inhabitants' (of Britain, that is).

Richard Morris was succeeded as president of the Cymmrodorion by Sir Watkin Lewes (1740–1821), a lawyer of Pembrokeshire origin who became Lord Mayor of London in 1780. Other prominent members of the society included Silvanus Bevan (1691–1765), a Quaker physician from Swansea, the poet Richard Fenton (1747–1821), and Joseph Harris (1704–64), who was assay-master at the Royal Mint. If you were a Welshman in London and hoped for royal favour, you could do no better than to join the Cymmrodorion. The society still exists today, with the prince of Wales as its patron.

One notable Welsh woman who could have been seen in London during the latter half of the eighteenth century was Hester Thrale, née Salisbury (1741–1821), another member of the Llewenni clan descended from Katheryn of Berain. Hester married Southwark brewer Henry Thrale in 1763 and the couple became friendly with Dr Samuel Johnson, who accompanied them on a tour of Wales in 1774. Later he came with them to France, where they saw the French king and queen, Louis XVI and Marie Antoinette, at Versailles. The sight seems to have impressed them, and Mrs Thrale, following the events of the French Revolution, felt some sympathy for Marie Antoinette. She nevertheless criticized the queen as being 'at the head of a set of monsters, call'd by each other Sapphists', a veiled reference to lesbian relationships.

Like most of her contemporaries, Hester Thrale took a keen interest in the activities of Britain's royal family. In 1761, aged 20, she wrote a poem in honour of the occasion of the marriage of the young King George III to Charlotte of Mecklenburg-Strelitz; seventeen years later she included it in her *Thraliana*. Could it be that the young Hester had herself nurtured a 'crush' on Britain's most eligible bachelor? The poem is eminently forgettable, but gushes in praise of the new queen in much the same way that royal-watchers of 1981 gushed over Lady Diana Spencer.

> She, fair, unaffected could conquer each Heart
> And wise without Cunning could please without Art;
> In private Life chearful, in Publick – serene;
> How sweet a Companion! how gracious a Queen!
> With Spirit good humour'd, with Modesty gay,
> Such the Daughter of Merit, the Queen of the May.

Mrs Thrale's letters and diaries report on such topics as the illness of the prince of Wales, and she records how she pestered her friend Dr Johnson for his memories of Queen Anne (who died when Johnson was 5 years old). By 1804, when a Napoleonic invasion threatened, Mrs Thrale was no longer as fond of the prince of Wales as she had been, reporting that 'we shall escape the horrors of a regency'. She writes like one who respects the royal family but no longer reveres it. By now she was married for the second time, to an Italian, and had retired to her native land of Wales.

There was another Welsh woman in Samuel Johnson's life. Anna Williams (1706–83) had come to London from Pembrokeshire with her father in the 1720s. Her writing and translations brought her into contact with Johnson, and he tried to help when she began going blind during the 1740s. Following her father's death, he and others supported Miss Williams financially, and she lived, on and off, in his household. In 1774, he helped her apply for support to a charity based at Christ's Hospital. The application failed because of her nationality. The Welsh might have thought they were accepted in England, but the kingdom was not quite as united as Dr Johnson had imagined.

The monarchy could hardly be blamed for the vagaries of a private charity. They continued to interest themselves in the principality from a distance. Books like Thomas Pennant's *Tours in Wales* (1778) were popular for the picture they painted of this quaint far-off land where bards had once been a feature of every prince's court. In 1775, Thomas Gray (better known for his *Elegy in a Country Churchyard*) wrote *The Bard*, a highly romanticized account of the last days of Welsh independence. In keeping with the theme, he attempted to persuade a friend to set it to music; nothing seems to have come of this plan.

In this poem, a bard curses the conquering Edward I with these words:

> 'Nor e'en thy virtues, tyrant, shall avail
> To save thy secret soul from nightly fears,
> From Cambria's curse, from Cambria's tears!'

Gray goes on to recite the awful deaths of Edward II, the Black Prince, Richard II and Henry VI, among others, before describing how the curse was broken by the advent of the Tudor dynasty. Gray, it seems, was familiar with the prophecy of the 'mab darogan'. When his book was reprinted during the reign of Queen Victoria, the verses relating to Elizabeth I gained a double meaning, as though Victoria herself were responsible for a triumphant reunion of Welsh and English. The kings and queens of the eighteenth and nineteenth centuries chose not to identify with the Plantagenets; the monarch's image was changing to that of an enlightened and benevolent administrator who governed by consensus.

Forty years later, Gray's poem was still well known enough for the Northumberland artist John Martin to attempt to represent it in oils. The last of the bards, a tiny figure on a lofty wooded crag, the wind blowing in his white hair, stands defiant with his harp, moments before throwing himself to his destruction. It is considered one of the most important paintings of the English Romantic movement and, though it may be considered a political statement, it is not overtly anti-royal.

Music was another aspect of Welsh culture that found its way into London society. Welsh harpists were popular with British rulers from the eighteenth century onwards. In 1805 the harpist Edward Jones (1752–1824) was given accommodation in St James's Palace, so that he could be on hand whenever he was needed. In 1820 Jones gained the epithet 'bardd y brenin' ('the king's bard'), when his long-standing patron, the prince of Wales, came to the throne as King George IV. Jones took pride in the title, continuing to use it until his dying day. The whimsical monarch may not have called on him frequently to play, but behind the appointment was a symbolism that is easy to comprehend. It helped maintain the image of the royal family as having a consciousness of the further reaches of their 'united' kingdom, even if they seldom visited these remote regions in person. More to the point, it enabled a sovereign whose powers were limited by Parliament to hark back to the days when the royal word was law and the bard's sole purpose was to sing his prince's praises.

This particular fashion never died out. In 1849, Ellis Roberts, known by the bardic name of 'Eos Meirion', was appointed harpist to the 8-year-old prince of Wales. This was just as well, since the prince had been presented with a six-foot Welsh harp two years earlier, following his visit to Wales. It was the time of a major Welsh cultural revival, involving figures such as Edward Williams (1747–1826), better known as Iolo Morganwg, and Gwallter Mechain (1761–1849). The first of Iolo's new-style eisteddfodau was held, not in Wales, but in London's Primrose Hill in 1792. London was taking the lead because it had a bigger concentration of Welsh people than most Welsh towns. That would change, as the Industrial Revolution caught hold, and Merthyr Tydfil, Cardiff, Swansea and Newport gradually became the most populous areas of Wales.

Iolo was not, however, a monarchist. He hoped for a return to the old regime (without being entirely sure what it was). In his *Ode on the Mythology of the Ancient British Bards*, which he recited at the Primrose Hill eisteddfod, he railed against 'tyrants'. At around the same time, another Welshman, the philosopher Richard Price (1723–91), was praising the American and French revolutionaries for rebelling against their respective monarchs. Some called this the Age of Enlightenment.

## ROYAL VISITS

The Welsh in Wales had to wait until the beginning of the nineteenth century for their first close encounter with the Hanoverian royal family. George III (proud of having been born in Britain, but not enough to visit Wales in person) appointed his brother, Prince William Henry, to the somewhat honorary position of governor of Chester and north Wales. Even so, it took until 1803 for the prince to get as far as Chester, let alone Wales.

George III's eldest son would, of course, become prince of Wales. Unlike his three immediate predecessors, this prince acquired the title as a baby, another indication of his father's determination to do his duty towards the people of Britain in the most formal sense. George IV actually visited Wales at least three times in his life, though only once as prince of Wales. This was in 1806, when he and his brother, Prince William, took up an offer from Sir Richard Puleston (1765–1819) to 'introduce' the prince of Wales into his principality. Sir Richard was a member of the family that had first settled in north Wales during the thirteenth century and might therefore be regarded as well integrated.

A few years earlier, Sir Richard had entertained another member of the royal family, Prince William Frederick, son of the duke of Gloucester. The duke himself had stayed with Sir Watkin Williams-Wynn (1772–1840) at Wynnstay (either not knowing or not caring about the involvement of Sir Watkin's grandfather with the Jacobite cause) before returning to Chester. Prince William Frederick, then in his twenties, remained in Wales for a few days, and was welcomed to Llewenni Hall, the home of John FitzMaurice, Viscount Kirkwall (1778–1820). Kirkwall, who was around the same age as his guest, ensured that the prince received a proper welcome, and dignitaries turned out from Denbigh to pay their respects. According to contemporary accounts, the young royal made an outstanding impression.

No doubt Sir Richard was recommended to the two princes by their cousin. Puleston had been married, for about six years, to his second wife Emma, a famous beauty. In view of the prince of Wales's reputation, she may well have been part of the motivation for his visit. The princes were visiting the Shropshire estate of Lotton Park when they made their impromptu decision to venture over the border. Puleston was the only Welshman present in the company at Lotton Park, and was therefore selected to accompany them. The prince of Wales, to mark the spot where he first set foot on the soil of his principality, planted a young oak tree. Although the ceremony must have been planned in advance by others, it was a gesture quite in keeping with George's sentimental nature. To underline his new-found affection for Wales, the prince took a sprig from the tree, placed it in his hat, and remarked that it was 'the proudest ornament he had ever worn'. As for his host, Sir Richard was given permission to add an oak tree and the three ostrich feathers of the prince of Wales's emblem to his own arms.

In 1821, George IV, having effectively been monarch since the start of his father's last illness ten years earlier, was finally crowned king. His coronation, as described by Sir Walter Scott, was the most magnificent in British history. The woman who should have been crowned queen, Caroline of Brunswick, had lived apart from her husband for many years, and arrived at Westminster Abbey to find herself excluded from the ceremony. Shortly after his accession, the king embarked on a tour of his realm. He had decided that he simply must visit Ireland, and what better way of getting there than on his yacht, the *Royal George*. A few days after leaving Portsmouth, the royal party arrived at Holyhead.

To this day, when the present queen arrives for an official visit, she will often find a red carpet laid out to await her. In George IV's case, the dignitaries of Holyhead had prepared a special landing stage, complete with triumphal arch and floral decorations. After hearing the loyal address, the king expressed his affection for Wales, 'a country which was, and always would be, dear to him'. A carriage awaited him, and, after a leisurely drive along the promenade, where throngs of local people cheered him, he was whisked off to Plas Newydd, the mansion owned by Henry Paget, marquess of Anglesey (1768–1854), a military hero who had lost his leg at the Battle of Waterloo.

Among the king's party was Lord Conyngham, the husband of the incumbent royal mistress. During dinner at Plas Newydd, news arrived that the unacknowledged queen, Caroline of Brunswick, was close to death. Though the king appeared subdued, he was secretly elated, telling Sir William Knighton that Caroline's death gave him 'a fair prospect of real and true happiness for the rest of my days'. When it was confirmed that Caroline had died, the king retreated from public view and was said to have 'dined alone' on board his yacht. For a social animal like George IV, this must have been quite a sacrifice. He could not risk appearing in public, lest his true feelings about his bereavement made themselves too apparent. The yacht remained in the harbour at Holyhead until the winds for Ireland were favourable. The day of his departure was the king's fifty-ninth birthday.

On his return from Ireland, the king's progress by sea was once again affected by the weather. This time he was forced to put into Milford Haven, on the southern coast of Wales, to await a change in the wind. On 13 September 1821, following three unsuccessful attempts to make progress, the king disembarked at Milford for a quick look round, an event that is commemorated in a stone subsequently erected by Robert Fulke Greville (1800–67), the town's effective owner. Greville's father and namesake had been an equerry to King George III. According to the inscription, the king was met with 'acclamations and shouts of welcome from thousands of his majesty's loyal and warm hearted Welsh subjects who from distant parts had hastened to the spot and now zealously united with the inhabitants of Milford and its neighbourhood in making on this joyful occasion a dutiful and affectionate homage to their beloved king'.

Plas Newydd would become a regular royal retreat, with Princess Victoria and her widowed mother, the duchess of Kent, spending some weeks there in 1832. In his *Topographical Dictionary of Wales* (1833), Samuel Lewis describes it as 'beautifully situated in a portion of the old Druidical groves, on ground rising gently from the margin of the Menai'. This fanciful description reflects the contemporary interest in the 'picturesque', fostered by travel writers such as William Gilpin, whose journey through the Wye valley in 1770 had been recorded for posterity.

In 1828, a major eisteddfod was held at Denbigh, and Prince Augustus Frederick, duke of Sussex, a younger brother of King George IV, happened to be at nearby Kinmel Park, where he was a regular visitor. On Wednesday, 17 September, he called in to see what all the fuss was about. A national eisteddfod was not yet an annual event, but the duke's visit attracted additional crowds. This eisteddfod came to be referred to as the 'Royal Denbigh Eisteddfod', long before the 'National Eisteddfod' officially existed.

The visit was not unexpected, and a deputation was sent to welcome the duke. The Corporation of Denbigh thanked him for 'so powerfully contributing to increase in splendour and effect those popular attractions which must ensure the eventual success, and thus promote the combined objects for which this and other meetings of a similar kind have been really revived'. The duke responded that he was 'delighted in being permitted to witness a scene which must be highly interesting to all well-wishers of their country'.

After a royal 'walkabout', the duke, seated on a platform in full view of the cheering crowds, was entertained by such great names as John Parry (1776–1851), the harpist and composer better known by his bardic name of 'Bardd Alaw'. Another harpist, Richard Roberts, won the contest for a gold harp, which was presented by the duke of Sussex himself. John Parry was a native of Denbigh, and was joined on the platform by another famous figure in the history of the arts in Wales: the Reverend Thomas Price (1787–1848). Price, better known by his bardic name of 'Carnhuanawc', was the mentor of Lady Charlotte Guest (1812–1895), the wife of the owner of Dowlais ironworks; Lady Charlotte rubbed shoulders with royalty and translated the Mabinogion into English. Another lady with whom Carnhuanawc worked closely was Lady Llanover (1802–96), now remembered chiefly as the 'inventor' of Welsh national costume.

The duke of Sussex was in his fifties at the time of his visit to the eisteddfod. His lifestyle was not one that would have appealed to the Nonconformists who made up a large proportion of ordinary eisteddfod-goers. As a young man, he had been married to Lady Augusta Murray, in contravention of the Royal Marriages Act of 1772 (which had been passed by the duke's father, King George III, originally in an unsuccessful attempt to bring his unruly brothers to heel). The marriage produced two children, but was annulled as soon as the duke's father found out about it; nevertheless, he had continued to live with the lady for several years afterwards. On the other hand, his marriage had been to a respectable woman, the daughter of an earl and, unlike his brother the king, he waited for his first wife to die before marrying a second time. Moreover, the fact that he had visited friends in Wales regularly gave him a better right to a warm reception in the principality than most members of the royal family.

Ten days after the eisteddfod festivities, a ball was held at Denbigh Town Hall in honour of the duke, giving an opportunity to the local gentry to see royalty at closer quarters. Sir Walter Scott, Robert Southey and William Wordsworth were all invited; none of them turned up. Those who did attend included the antiquary Angharad Llwyd (1780–1866), the Reverend Samuel Roberts of Llanbrynmair (1800–85) and Robert Davies (1769–1835), better known as 'Bardd Nantglyn'. All were awarded silver medals in recognition of their services to the arts in Wales.

In the twentieth century, as might be expected, the most frequent visitor to Wales has been its present prince. Perhaps as a result of nationalist activity, visits from the reigning monarch have also increased in frequency during the past fifty years. The late Queen Mother was a favourite with the Welsh public, though perhaps no more so than she was with the rest of the UK. She had already enjoyed their generosity in 1923, when, as Lady Elizabeth Bowes-Lyon, she married the duke of York and was presented with a nugget of gold from the Clogau mine at Bontddu from which her wedding ring was made. The wedding rings worn by the present queen, Princess Margaret and several other royal brides have come from that same nugget.

In 1937, shortly after being thrust into the limelight by the abdication of Edward VIII, the former duchess and her husband, now elevated to the throne as King George VI, arrived in Aberystwyth to open the new National Library of Wales building. It was their first engagement in Wales since the king's accession, but Queen Elizabeth would visit many more times during her long life. One of her last visits was, fittingly, to view the 'George Thomas Suite' at Cardiff Castle. Thomas, elevated late in life to the title of Viscount Tonypandy, was considered a close friend.

The present queen, naturally, is also a regular visitor. Independent Television maintains an archive of film clips on its website, showing the Queen at all stages of her career, from her Coronation Tour of 1953 right up to the present day, including film of at least thirty-five official visits within the principality. One of the most memorable is the film of an ashen-faced Elizabeth II arriving at Aberfan a few days after the disaster of October 1966. She is said to have wept while talking to bereaved mothers, a normal human reaction but one which we somehow do not expect of our monarch.

Someone with royal associations who was also present at Aberfan was George Thomas, soon to be Secretary of State for Wales. Although a single man with no children of his own, he managed to capture the mood of the day. His sentimental brand of Christianity seemed to be what the ordinary people of Aberfan needed at the moment of disaster. It was he who showed the Queen the scene of the landslide, reporting later on her reactions. Thomas, suffering the same fluctuations in his popularity as any royal, was later described as 'absurd' and 'despicable' for participating in the Government's penny-pinching policy over the removal of the coal tips.

The question of what royal visits nowadays actually mean to the people of Wales is a difficult one. Crowds gather to see them, but they are rarely any bigger or more enthusiastic than the crowds attracted by many visiting celebrities. The main difference is that the opportunity to see the royals arrive carries no admission fee, provided one is willing to wait at the roadside for long enough. Diana, princess of Wales, was the only member of the royal family in recent years who had the kind of celebrity appeal that might be commanded by a rock singer or film star, and it was not reserved for any particular section of the public. Young and old alike would flock to see Diana because she was physically attractive, elegant *and* had a warm and welcoming personality. Yet her glamour was preserved within an aura of humanity. Had Diana been around at the time of the Aberfan disaster, we can be sure that she would have been one of the first visitors on the scene. Onlookers would have *expected* to see her cry.

It takes more than being royal to win public acclaim, and the flags waved and cheers raised when the Queen drives by in her limousine often owe more to a sense of duty, or perhaps even to curiosity, than to any genuine personal affection. In this respect, our attitude to the royals has not changed significantly since the Middle Ages.


## THE LANGUAGE

The Welsh language is the cultural banner of the principality, our one unquestioned success story. It is the envy of other small states, particularly the Celtic nations. Even those who cannot speak it are proud of it. Even those who mock it are jealous of those who can speak it.

Contrary to what many people believe, the Welsh language was not brought to the verge of extinction by the conquest of Edward I. It continued to thrive for centuries afterwards, right up to the present day. The activities of those Victorian schoolmasters who tried to prevent Welsh pupils from using their native language in classroom and playground were not actively condoned by Britain's royal family, even if the Welsh language was generally despised throughout the rest of the kingdom.

What may fairly be said, however, is that the British royal family (apart from the present prince of Wales and his first wife) have never gone out of their way to learn Welsh. It is a matter for speculation whether those English kings who were born or spent time in Wales, such as Henry V and Henry VII, were familiar with the language (which, unlike English, is little changed since the Middle Ages). Since the mass media began to take an interest in such things, however, there have been some notable statements on the subject.

Dr John Davies of Mallwyd (d.1644) was an early proponent of the idea that the prince of Wales should be able to communicate with his subjects in their own tongue. The idea did not take off on that occasion. Davies, an Oxford graduate, is thought to have assisted in the translation of Bishop Parry's 1620 Welsh Bible. He published a grammar of the *Antiquae Linguae Britannicae* (i.e. Welsh) in the following year, and followed it up with a Welsh–Latin dictionary in 1632. Like his namesake and contemporary, John Davies of Hereford, Dr Davies was given to the popular practice of dedicating his published work to members of the royal family.

Davies believed that the Welsh language was as ancient as any known language of its time, having been spoken in the British Isles in the days when 'Brutus' (a legendary survivor of the Trojan War) arrived there. He, and other Welsh writers, listed the twenty-four 'measures of a man', which included such skills as hunting, archery *and* the ability to read Welsh! It was no wonder, then, that he proposed the prince of Wales (by this time Charles Stuart, son of King Charles I) should learn the language.

The proposal was repeated during the nineteenth century, in relation to the new prince, the future Edward VII, and was met with derision. A correspondent of the *Cambrian* newspaper warned of the danger that the prince, in trying to pronounce the more difficult Welsh sounds, would be mistaken for someone in the throes of 'quinsy or some terrible disease of the lungs and jugulum'.

More than three centuries after John Davies's proposal, the soon-to-be-invested Charles Windsor took a term off from his Cambridge undergraduate course to study Welsh at the University of Wales in Aberystwyth. His 1969 stay was the occasion for student protests which saw many Welsh-speaking students taking the prince's side. Charles might have been ridiculed for his position and background, but he could hardly be criticized for showing a willingness to learn the language.

Charles's predecessor, Edward VIII, had been taught a few words of Welsh by David Lloyd George, to enable him to make a very short speech at his investiture of 1911, but Charles was keen to *understand* what he was saying as well as to pronounce it properly. His elder son William, assumed by many to be the next prince of Wales, is also taking Welsh lessons. William himself has described his command of the language as 'poor'.

## CHANGING ATTITUDES?

Supremacy was no longer decided solely by blood and descent, and thus the royal family had largely ceased to be the primary target for popular discontent. A curious result of this was that gradually, as kings and queens began to show more understanding of, and more sympathy with, their subjects, those subjects began to identify more with their royals. Queen Victoria might have written condescendingly that the Welsh were 'naturally sensitive and warmhearted people', but at the same time a Welshman could write that the queen was 'among the most accomplished ladies in her dominions', and expect her to take it as a compliment. Earlier monarchs had not *always* been remote from their subjects, but by the twentieth century the prevalent attitude of the people towards their rulers was no longer one of fear and abasement but one of outspoken criticism alternating with something verging on pity.

This does not mean that *some* Welsh men and women did not continue to have an almost unhealthy degree of respect for those they considered their betters on the grounds of birth. Take George Thomas, Viscount Tonypandy. Despite his socialist convictions, Thomas was a particular admirer of the late Queen Mother, and commented approvingly that she had brought 'all the breeziness of the Scots, the warmth of heart of a Celt' into the royal family. Elizabeth Bowes-Lyon was indeed of Scots parentage, but she was born in London and brought up at her parents' home in Hertfordshire as well as at Glamis Castle in Scotland.

George Thomas recalled that he had once brought her a present of a red glass dragon, from a craft shop in Cardiff. Years later, when he visited her at Clarence House, he saw the dragon prominently displayed. His hostess hastened to assure him that she had not put out the ornament specially, simply because he was coming. 'It's always there', she insisted, almost as though *she* were looking for *his* approval, rather than the other way round; and this was, perhaps, the case. The royal family, once absolute power was taken away from them, felt the need to seek approval from their subjects for their actions, if only so as to maintain their position. This has not changed.

Whether the Welsh have any specific status in this context is difficult to see, but two special observations may reasonably be made about Wales's relationship with royalty. One is that the British monarchy is repeatedly made to feel guilty about, and even responsible for, the past actions of English kings in respect of Wales (this is of course also true of Scotland and Ireland). Henry Tudor's position in the league table of British rulers somehow becomes almost insignificant in the popular view, when measured against the perceived tyranny of Edward I.

The second point to note is the unique position of the prince of Wales. There are other examples of titles given to the eldest sons of monarchs that have a comparable significance. For example, the heir to the kingdom of Spain is the prince of Asturias (Asturias referring to a former independent kingdom on Spain's northern coast). However, the latter title was in fact developed during the fourteenth century using the title of prince of Wales as a model. In a British context, the prince of Wales is seen as a monarch in the process of being prepared for his future station. The principality is his training ground. Although the heir to the throne has English and Scottish titles, and indeed is known as 'the duke of Rothesay' when he is in Scotland, it is as prince of Wales that he is universally recognized.

Conversely, it is only through the title prince of Wales that the word 'Wales' is familiar worldwide. This has been the case for some centuries, and Wales's global profile has risen and fallen depending on the profile of the incumbent prince. With the coming (and departure) of Diana, princess of Wales, the name of the principality gained an additional resonance, but lost even more of its primary meaning. As a result of her activities, the name of Wales gained a 'good' connotation which was not lost even when her image became tarnished, so completely did she become identified with her title. The prince of Wales has not made quite the same impact on the world. This could easily change, and undoubtedly will change, with future princes and princesses.

# Victorians and Edwardians

In contrast to her famous love of Scotland, Queen Victoria did not show any great interest in, or affection for, Wales. She visited for the first time before she came to the throne, during the reign of her uncle and predecessor, King William IV. William, the oldest king ever to arrive on the British throne (he was 64 at the time of his accession, setting a record that not even Edward VII could equal), enjoyed public adulation. William and his wife, Queen Adelaide, were so thrilled at their unexpected advancement that they would sometimes descend from their carriage in the London streets to accept the plaudits of the crowds at close hand. Yet his sole visit to Wales had been marred by what he considered excessive enthusiasm.

Victoria, an impressionable teenager, was accompanied by her mother, the duchess of Kent. The duchess, originally Princess Victoria of Saxe-Coburg-Saalfeld, had married Charles, prince of Leiningen, at the age of 17 (her groom was 40). She had two children from this first marriage. Following the prince's death, his nubile widow married Edward, duke of Kent, a younger son of King George III. Victoria was their only child.

The duke of Kent died suddenly in 1820, when his daughter was less than a year old. One of those who missed him most was the social reformer and inventor of the Co-operative Society, Robert Owen (1771–1858) who, despite his own socialist leanings, had gained a valuable ally in the duke. When Owen travelled to France in 1817, spreading his ideas, he took with him a letter of introduction from the duke of Kent to the duc d'Orléans.

Widowed for a second time, the duchess began to depend heavily on her private secretary, John Conroy, an Irishman who was not popular with the rest of the royal family. Soon, under Conroy's influence, she virtually cut off relations with her brother-in-law King William IV, who came to the throne in 1830. Princess Victoria, no doubt feeling excluded from her mother's affection, turned to her governess, the redoubtable Baroness Lehzen. Thus Victoria's relationship with her mother, even at the time of their Welsh visit, was far from straightforward.

Both Lehzen and Conroy accompanied the duchess of Kent and her daughter to Wales in 1832. The ostensible purpose of the young princess's visit, which was part of a 'progress' throughout England and Wales, was to acquaint herself with her future realm. Local dignitaries would have been quite aware that, in the event of the princess acceding to the throne before she reached her majority, her mother was likely to become regent. Thus the duchess was assured of an enthusiastic welcome, equal to that received by the princess. She ingratiated herself further by presenting £100 to the local authorities in Welshpool, a donation towards the upkeep of schools in the area. Similar donations were made to other local charities.

It was a lengthy visit, including a reception at Shrewsbury, where, among other things, the heir to the throne was presented with a box of 'Shrewsbury cakes'. More gifts would be pressed upon young Victoria during her stay in Wales, including a wooden doll in Welsh costume and a volume entitled *History of Oswestry*, the latter presented to her by its author, a Mr Minshull. The doll made a temporary return to the principality in an exhibition at the National Library of Wales during 2008. Victoria seems to have been quite taken with the Welsh costume, commenting in her diary that 'All the young women are very pretty, and they all wear hats; it looks so funny to see them come out of their cottages, knitting, with little white caps, black hats, yellow handkerchieves, and blue petticoats.' The doll was added to the 132 that the princess already owned.

Unsolicited gifts such as these were as common during royal visits then as they are now; it is hardly any wonder that Victoria lost her youthful figure so quickly if she was expected to sample and express appreciation of regional foods every time she arrived for an official visit. (In the twentieth century, a royal princess would become seriously ill as a result of trying to preserve her elegant appearance whilst having excessive hospitality thrust upon her.) By the time Victoria completed her progress around England and Wales, she must have been heartily sick of it all, and the regions of her kingdom must have begun to blur into one. When she visited Wales to celebrate her golden jubilee, it would be clear that she had little recollection of the places she had stayed in 1832.

In August the princess and her mother were due to visit Beaumaris Castle, where an eisteddfod was taking place, but were deterred from actual attendance by the weather. Eisteddfod prize-winners, including the noted bard 'Caledfryn' (real name William Williams), who won the chair on that occasion, were obliged to travel to the Bulkeleys' nearby seat of Baron Hill to meet Victoria and her mother. The presentation had to be carried out on the terrace outside the house, so great was the crowd that had assembled in the hope of seeing them. A medal presented by the princess on that occasion can be seen in the National Museum of Wales.

The management of the Bulkeley Hotel in Beaumaris make the proud claim that the future queen slept there on 8 August 1832, before being scared away by rumours of a cholera outbreak. The hotel had been erected only three years earlier, apparently in expectation of a future royal visit. At the time of Victoria's arrival, it was the venue for a lavish party to celebrate the marriage of Sir Richard Bulkeley Williams-Bulkeley (1801–75), scion of the illustrious Bulkeley family that had been prominent in Anglesey since Tudor times. The hotel landlady, one Mrs Bicknell, waited on the royal party, and, after settling into their accommodation, the princess and her mother went out onto the portico of the hotel to wave to cheering crowds.

Other great houses visited by Victoria during that stay in north Wales included Wynnstay and Powis Castle. At the latter, she was entertained by the second earl, Edward Herbert. Herbert's loyalty to the royal family was not perhaps as unquestioning as that of some of his predecessors. He would later be Prince Albert's rival for the chancellorship of the University of Cambridge. Nevertheless, his Powis estate was a pleasant place for a royal stopover, unrivalled as a venue for hunting, shooting and fishing. Here, in 1848, the earl would be accidentally shot dead by one of his own sons.

The royal party also passed through Chirk, and admired two feats of engineering for which north Wales is still famous: the Pontcysyllte Aqueduct on the Llangollen Canal (completed in 1805 by Thomas Telford and William Jessop) and Telford's suspension bridge over the Menai Strait, opened only six years before Victoria's visit. Conroy was anxious to escort the princess through Caernarfon Castle so that she could see for herself the chamber where the first English prince of Wales was said to have been born. The duchess's response to the greetings of the burgesses of Caernarfon suggest she was a little peeved that the 'private visit' to the castle had been subject to so much publicity; or perhaps she was being disingenuous.

All this excitement was too much for the princess, who did not appear the following day for the planned outing on Lake Llanberis. The obvious disappointment of the crowds must have been irksome to the duchess, who took it on herself to speak for her daughter even when the latter was present. Nevertheless, Victoria's mother was the centre of attention a few days later, when her birthday was celebrated at Beaumaris, Sir Richard Bulkeley himself hosting the festivities.

Later in the week the party would visit Conway Castle and steam around the island of Anglesey in various pleasure-craft supplied by the local nobility, including the *Menai*, on board which they were given dinner by Thomas Assheton Smith (1752–1828), a notable cricketer and owner of the Faenol estate, where Bryn Terfel now holds his annual music festival.

The Bulkeley family later claimed that the cholera scare which caused the royals to cut short their stay in Beaumaris town had been blown out of all proportion by the marquess of Anglesey. The latter was keen to see Victoria and her mother as his own guests, and indeed the royal party soon took refuge at Plas Newydd, the house that had entertained her uncle, King George IV, a few years earlier. Lovely as the landscape may have been, Victoria's first visit would not make a permanent impression on the nature-loving queen. On a later visit to the principality, as she recorded in her diary, she needed to be reminded of some of the places where she had stayed first time round.

Victoria and her entourage remained at Plas Newydd until October, when they departed from Wales, travelling via Abergele, Kinmel Park, St Asaph and Holywell. One of their overnight stops was at Hawarden, home of Sir Stephen Glynne, the 9th baronet (1807–74), who had just been elected to Parliament. The baronet was not at home, and the royals were received by the Reverend George Neville Grenville, later dean of Windsor, who was occupying the house at the time. Sir Stephen's sister would later enjoy some prominence in royal circles, through her marriage to one of Victoria's most famous prime ministers.

Along their route, the royal party were met by bishops, baronets and armed escorts of various kinds, not to mention the ubiquitous crowds of ordinary well-wishers. It was easy for the Welsh people to take the tiny 13-year-old princess to their hearts; no one could possibly see her as an instrument of English oppression. Any nationalistic feeling that might have been germinating was nipped in the bud. What the people did not realize was the way their emotional and enthusiastic response to the little princess was being manipulated by the duchess of Kent and Sir John Conroy. They were effectively setting up a rival royal family, much as Hanoverian heirs to the British throne had done during the previous century.

Victoria would not see Wales again for many years, nor would she appear greatly concerned by its political and social problems. Chartism became a growing movement in the early years of her reign, and in November 1839 John Frost (1784–1877) led a march on Newport which resulted in Frost himself and two other prominent Chartists being convicted of treason and transported to Australia. Events in Wales were only too typical of what was happening in the country as a whole, and in 1848, at the height of the national movement, the queen was evacuated to the Isle of Wight for her own safety.

Fear of political unrest was not a reason for avoiding Wales. The year after the Newport 'Rising', Victoria married her cousin Albert. Early in their married life, the royal couple and their children passed through the principality, but did not stay long. On 11 August 1847, the queen,

Prince Albert, their son Bertie (already invested as prince of Wales) and their daughter Vicky anchored off Milford Haven in the royal yacht, en route from the Scilly Isles to Scotland. Victoria, who had been very seasick during the voyage, did not even disembark, but stayed on deck, 'sketching', while her husband visited Pembroke in the company of Victoria's older half-brother, Carl, prince of Leiningen.

The next port of call was Caernarfon, where Victoria had visited the castle fifteen years earlier. This time the queen was doubly welcome because of the presence of the little prince of Wales in the party. Portraits of Bertie in the sailor suit he wore during his Welsh visit reveal that he was much better looking as a small child than he was to be as an adult. Local dignitaries were as eager to greet him as they had been to greet Victoria when she was heir to the throne. The only person more attractive to favour-seekers than the present monarch is a future monarch. The captain of a passenger steamer named *Prince of Wales* made a special request to be allowed a glimpse of *the* prince of Wales, and was allowed the privilege.

Meanwhile, the prince consort, making a show of his intellectual ability as always, headed for the Menai Bridge to admire its engineering, and travelled from there to Penrhyn Castle. The crowds who had gathered on the quaysides in the hope of seeing the queen, however, were mostly disappointed. The royal yacht shot past Beaumaris in the dusk, and few caught sight of Victoria herself, waving graciously from the deck.

Other members of the royal family visited Wales. It was a popular tourist destination and, despite the adulation, it was still somewhere that a royal could enjoy a little peace and seclusion. In 1849, Princess Mary Adelaide visited north Wales in the company of her father and brother. She was 15 years old at the time. Her father, Prince Adolphus, duke of Cambridge, was a son of King George III. Mary Adelaide's daughter would one day be queen.

When Prince Adolphus died, the following year, his widow, Princess Augusta (another princess of German origin), expressed her intention of relocating to Wales to live. It was rumoured that the duchess would have as her official residence Plas Newydd, the mansion on the banks of the Menai Strait owned by the marquess of Anglesey and visited by so many royals before her. We can imagine the excitement in the hearts of the local population: the prospects for the tradesmen, the possibility of other royals being attracted to the area or at least coming to visit. Needless to say, it never happened.

In the years of her absence from Wales, Victoria did not cease to have dealings with the Welsh. One Welshman who was knighted for his services to her was Sir Pryce Pryce-Jones (1834–1920), one of the first retailers to offer a mail order service. Victoria bought most of her underwear from him; it was made from Welsh flannel. Another Welsh knight of her early reign was Sir David Davies (1792–1865), who had been physician to King William IV and Queen Adelaide. His near-namesake, Sir David Daniel Davis (1777–1841), had actually been in attendance on the duchess of Kent at Victoria's birth. Much later in the century, another Welsh obstetrician, Sir John Williams (1840–1926), would continue the tradition of service to the royal family, and would be created a baronet by the queen.

William Ewart Gladstone was probably Victoria's least favourite of the eleven prime ministers she had in the course of her sixty-four-year reign. 'He speaks to me as if I was a public meeting', she famously commented to explain her dislike. Many contemporaries noted that Gladstone had the utmost respect for the monarchy. According to his biographer, John Morley, the politician's greatest mistake in dealing with the queen was that 'his very awe of the institution made him set an exacting standard for the individual who represented it', one which Victoria perhaps realized she was unable to live up to.

It was Gladstone who proved the most sympathetic of all the Victorian prime ministers to the plight of the Welsh. This was due in no small measure to his personal familiarity with Wales and its people. In 1839 he had married Catherine Glynne of Hawarden (1812–1900), and he spent much of his leisure time at her family seat, where he eventually retired. When new bishops needed to be appointed to dioceses in Wales, Gladstone took it upon himself to ensure that the individuals appointed were Welsh speakers or at least had an understanding of the locality. Through the Irish Home Rule Bills he tried so hard to pass, in 1886 and 1893, Gladstone also laid the foundations for devolution. It was Gladstone's Liberal Party that made possible the disestablishment of the Church in Wales, though the latter measure was carried through by one of his successors, David Lloyd George (1863–1945).

By such actions Gladstone made himself unpopular with other politicians, especially those of a unionist persuasion. One of his opponents, J. E. Vincent, writing in *The Times*, said that no one 'has ever exercised so much influence over Welsh minds as Mr Gladstone possesses'. He accused Gladstone of stirring up 'nationalistic aspirations in the Principality'. We may surmise that the queen was equally unamused at the prospect of losing such a large chunk of her realm, and perhaps it was partly this fear that encouraged her visit of 1889, only the second she had made since coming to the throne.

The royal party passed through Llangollen, and had tea with Sir Theodore and Lady Martin at Bryntisilio. Sir Theodore, as Prince Albert's biographer, was in good favour with the queen; and his wife, the former Helena Faucit, had been a celebrated actress before their marriage. Here Victoria was entertained by massed local choirs. The old queen, with all her usual condescension, commented that 'It is wonderful how well these choirs sing, being composed merely of shopkeepers and flannel weavers.'

The following day, 27 August 1889, the queen and her retinue were still in the area, their hosts being the owners of Palé Hall, a mansion in Llanderfel. It was a relatively new house, having been built around 1870 for a Scots industrialist, Henry Robertson, by a Shrewsbury architect, Samuel Pountney Smith. Robertson had died the year before Victoria's visit, and his son, the engineer Sir Henry Beyer Robertson, now owned the house. The queen is said to have been 'enchanted' by the place, and particularly enjoyed a walk along the bank of the River Dee; the route has been named Queen's Walk in memory of the occasion. Even the bath and bed used by Victoria during her stay have been preserved for posterity in what is now, aptly, a luxury hotel.

Following the death of the prince consort, Victoria had withdrawn from public life, and her son and daughter-in-law, the prince and princess of Wales, had to a great extent taken on the role of the public face of the royal family. The prince's wedding arrangements in 1863 were criticized, not for their lavishness, but for the failure to take into account the public's eagerness to be able to witness the celebrations. Rather than being held in central London, the wedding took place at St George's Chapel, Windsor, and the young couple (Alexandra was only 18) were obliged to run the gauntlet of well-wishers almost every time they went outside the door. During the post-wedding festivities in London, the crowds were so uncontrollable that six people were crushed to death.

Royal weddings were celebrated in Wales, just as they are now, but the cause for celebration was particularly great when it was the prince of Wales who was getting married. Most Welsh people could not hope to see the royal couple in person, but they could buy souvenirs of the event, such as china jugs and ornaments bearing pictures of the couple. They found other ways of marking the occasion, too: the popular song 'God Bless the Prince of Wales' was written in honour of the event. The next time an incumbent Prince of Wales would get married was in 1981, and most readers will recall what an impact that made on the public consciousness.

The next major royal wedding was in 1893, when the future prince of Wales and King George V married Princess Mary (or 'May') of Teck, the daughter of Princess Mary Adelaide. The bride had previously been engaged to the groom's elder brother, the late Prince Albert Victor, duke of Clarence. The older prince had been an unsteady sort, though adored by his mother, Alexandra, and there must have been a certain amount of relief in some quarters when he died suddenly of influenza, aged only 28. George, though just as academically unaccomplished as his brother, was regarded as more reliable and was considered to have higher moral standards.

The decision to make the wedding ring out of Welsh gold was not taken solely because George could expect to become prince of Wales as soon as his aged grandmother passed away. It was just one move in a determined campaign by the royal family to show how British they were. The public had not forgotten that the House of Saxe-Coburg-Gotha had originated in Germany, and that all royal consorts since the Hanoverian succession had come from roughly the same region of Europe. Victoria's husband, Albert, had been regarded with some suspicion on account of his place of birth. Now at last the people had a future queen who, despite her German roots, had actually been born in the UK. What better opportunity for the royal family to show its commitment to its adoptive country?

In June 1896, the prince and princess of Wales paid one of their rare visits to Wales. Reproved by his mother for not spending enough time in his principality, the long-serving 'Bertie' (later King Edward VII), was making up for lost time; he had visited only two years earlier, to be inducted into the Gorsedd at the National Eisteddfod. On this follow-up visit, he was installed as the chancellor of the University of Wales, and in succeeding years it became traditional for the current incumbent of the title prince of Wales to hold the chancellorship. The prince's first act was to invest his wife, Alexandra of Denmark, with an honorary degree, which may be considered ironic in view of the fact that he considered her too unintelligent to be allowed to look at any official papers.

Writing of the occasion in the magazine *Wales*, Owen M. Edwards describes it as 'a day which saw perfect unity of Welsh purpose'. William Gladstone was one of those who received honorary degrees alongside Alexandra. Edwards praises Gladstone, and it is evident that the prince of Wales had more respect for the old man than did his mother, the queen. He described the conferring of a degree on Gladstone as a privilege and a great honour for himself. It is clear from Edwards's comments that he regards the royal presence and the placing of the chancellorship in the hands of the prince of Wales as being essential to give the university the status it deserved. Later generations did not necessarily agree, and in 1976 the present prince was challenged unsuccessfully in the election for chancellor by veteran miners' leader Dai Francis.

During their 1896 visit to Wales, the princess of Wales opened a new pier pavilion at Aberystwyth. A funicular railway opened on the seafront in the same year, to carry the tourists attracted by the royal connection.

The prince and princess also visited Cardiff, to see the 'Fine Art, Industrial and Maritime Exhibition', and were filmed arriving by photographer Birt Acres. The film was one of the first of its kind and had to be taken to Buckingham Palace for an action replay.

In the following year, Queen Victoria celebrated her diamond jubilee, and the people of Wales seem to have been as enthusiastic as any other part of Britain about the opportunity to commemorate the occasion. The Powysland Museum in Welshpool possesses a photograph recording the imaginative efforts of a local person to mark the jubilee by decorating a bicycle with flowers.

No longer was Wales being completely ignored by the royal family. In 1906, another prince of Wales, the future George V, came to Cardiff to lay the foundation stone of the new university. He had succeeded his father both as prince of Wales and as chancellor of the University of Wales. Cardiff had, in the previous autumn, been made a city by the king. though it would be another fifty years before it became the official capital of Wales.

Although the former prince of Wales (still the longest-serving holder of the title) never gave the principality the same attention he gave to other parts of his mother's empire, he was no stranger to it. As king, Edward made a point of touring the British Isles on the royal yacht, the *Victoria and Albert*, a successor of the vessel from which he had first seen the coast of Wales as a small child. On one occasion, he disembarked unexpectedly at Pembroke Dock, and was taken by carriage to Pembroke Castle, where he visited local antiquarian J. R. Cobb, who had spent some years on a restoration project there. The story is still told by Pembroke Dock residents of how one excited local farmer fetched his pig and sat it on the wall beside him, to ensure that the animal did not miss the sight of the king passing through the town.

In 1907, the king, with Queen Alexandra and their daughter, the 40-year-old unmarried Princess Victoria, paid another official visit to Cardiff, this time to open the Alexandra Dock. The naming of the new dock was of course intended as a compliment to the queen, and commemorated the occasion permanently. Alexandra, a keen amateur photographer, took her own snaps of the event. Despite the many changes to Cardiff's profile in the intervening century, the dock is still in use.

## POLITICS

When the king and queen visited Cardiff in 1907, it was largely at the instigation of David Lloyd George, who was at the time president of the Board of Trade. The king is said to have remarked beforehand that 'nothing will induce him to visit Cardiff unless Mr Lloyd George learns how to behave with propriety'. None of the royal family ever took to Lloyd George, possibly because of his habit of playing to the gallery or perhaps because of his skill in manoeuvring the royals into courses of action that went against the grain. Lloyd George's opinion of them seems to have been equally low, though he disguised it well in public.

The turn of the twentieth century was probably the last time a British monarch willingly involved himself in politics. Although Edward VII was not exactly a political activist, he did take an interest in international affairs, and tended to side with his wife's anti-German family against his mother's Prussian relatives during periods of friction between the two. He was also instrumental in the signing of the 'entente cordiale' with France in 1904.

By the time Edward's son, as King George V, visited south Wales in 1912, Lloyd George had risen to the position of Chancellor of the Exchequer. Although as unpopular as ever with the king and queen, he had an uncanny ability to influence their activities. In 1911, he had persuaded them to agree to an investiture ceremony at Caernarfon Castle where the heir to the throne was invested with the title of prince of Wales amid great pomp and pageantry.

By the following year, when the king and queen decided to visit Dowlais ironworks, the political undercurrents brewing in the industrial valleys of the south had bubbled up, resulting in strikes and protests. Keir Hardie, Labour MP for Merthyr Tydfil, wrote to the *Merthyr Pioneer* to warn the royal couple of the dangers of going ahead with the visit. He even recommended that the king should 'boldly take your stand on the side of the workers' in order to win the approval of the Welsh people.

George V and his queen evidently knew more about the psyche of working-class people than Keir Hardie did. Naturally they were welcomed with open arms when, in June 1912, they visited Cardiff and the valleys. On 27 June, they travelled by royal train to Pontypridd, and were then driven through the Rhondda valley to Merthyr itself. At Aberdare they visited a miner's cottage, ostensibly to see for themselves the conditions in which their loyal subjects lived. The royal visit turned into a nice little earner for Mr and Mrs Jones, the tenants of the cottage, when sightseers, queuing up for a look at the teacup from which Queen Mary herself had drunk, were encouraged to fill it with loose change 'for the baby'.

The king and queen did of course visit Dowlais, completely ignoring Keir Hardie's advice (if indeed they had ever learned of his comments). It had never been an option for them to snub Britain's leading industrialists, a major source of the country's wealth, by calling off the visit. The royal couple opened a new blast engine house within the ironworks, and visited the owners at Dowlais House.

The fact that the south Wales valleys have in recent years become a bastion of Plaid Cymru voters did not prevent Merthyr Tydfil Heritage Trust, in 2007, from applying to the National Assembly for Wales for a grant to enable them to reconstruct the famous 'coal arch'. This somewhat unique structure had been erected at the entrance to Dowlais House to honour the king and queen on the day of their visit in 1912, and the trust hoped to replace it on its original site (despite the fact that Dowlais House was demolished in 1972). The stated purpose of the reconstruction project was 'to remind the community, especially our children, of the area's unique place in the creation of the modern world'; for the arch had been built by master craftsmen to emphasize Merthyr's leading role as a centre of the coal and iron industries.

# Residence in Wales

In 2007, the news that the prince of Wales was purchasing a house in the principality raised a few eyebrows. Prince Charles had briefly stayed in the celebrated Neuadd Pantycelyn, a student hall of residence, in Aberystwyth during 1969, but this was the nearest he had ever come to living in Wales. He does not, of course, plan to spend significant amounts of time in his new property near Llandovery. His plans to extend the property have aroused the indignation of local residents, but it is evident that the long-term plan is to add the dwellings on the Llwynwormwood estate to the portfolio of holiday properties already managed by the Duchy of Cornwall. It is doubtful whether the prince's sons and their girlfriends will be among those taking the cottages for a week in the summer. This is one respect in which the prince of Wales has failed to improve on the performance of his predecessors.

Histories of England tend to give the impression that there were no castles in Wales before Edward I built them. This is quite untrue. The Welsh princes built many castles, and stone ones at that, in the pre-conquest period. Their castles were not as grand as the Norman castles, nor as strong, because they did not have such large households and garrisons, and their enemies were not as numerous.

Llywelyn Fawr was the most active of these native Welsh castle-builders, throwing up new fortifications at Castell y Bere, Criccieth, Deganwy, Dolbadarn and Dolwyddelan. They were defensive structures, not primarily intended for living in. Llywelyn's court was peripatetic, moving between more pleasant living accommodations in places such as Aber Garth Celyn on the Menai Strait.

During the 1980s, an Elizabethan manor house called Pen-y-Bryn, in the village of Abergwyngregyn, began to attract attention from historians and archaeologists as a result of its residents' claim that it was the location of Llywelyn Fawr's palace of Aber. One part of the building has always been known by locals as 'Llywelyn's tower', but its historical significance was overlooked for many centuries. Evidence is mounting that this was indeed the place where Llywelyn and his wife Joan enjoyed their happiest and most peaceful days.

To reinforce his hold on the principality, Edward I built a string of castles across north Wales, designed by the Savoyard architect, Master James of St George. They were the most ambitious construction projects ever undertaken in Britain, but the king spent little time in any of them. The royal website claims Caernarfon Castle as a 'royal residence'. The king's son, the future Edward II, was born there, the occasion being commemorated in the name of Queen Eleanor's Gate, through which the prince's mother passed when she arrived, heavily pregnant, in the spring of 1284. Eleanor has the reputation of having introduced the use of tapestries as wall-hangings into England; and they would have been badly needed to bring warmth to the small chamber in which she is supposed to have given birth.

Caernarfon may have been a royal residence, but it was only one of many such places the queen and royal children found themselves forced to make the best of. In later years, at least one English king found it extremely uncomfortable. As we have already heard, Richard II, abandoned by most of his supporters, spent several dismal nights sleeping on straw in the semi-deserted castle before going to meet his doom at the hands of Henry Bolingbroke.

After the birth of the future Edward II, his parents moved on to hold court at Llywelyn's former palace of Garth Celyn, an action which signified the king's taking possession of Wales. Edward allegedly appropriated the crown jewels of Gwynedd, and the coronet of the princes of Wales, whose fate is unknown, has acquired almost mythical status. Like the Stone of Scone, it was a symbol of opposition which the English king would not tolerate.

The royal family spent some time at Conway, where once again the queen's reputed bedchamber has been identified and has its own private nook where Eleanor may have sat to look out at the best view in town. The royal party spent Christmas at Conway, and their visit is recorded in detail in John Stow's *Annals*, published nearly three hundred years later. Stow did not need to invent all the details, for records of royal expenditure and activities were generally kept, many of which are still available.

Since Wales lost its independence following the deaths of Llywelyn ap Gruffydd and his brother Dafydd, there has never been an *official* royal residence in Wales. The nearest thing to it was probably Ludlow Castle, where King Edward IV set up the Council of Wales and the Marches. Kings did not live at Ludlow, but several princes spent time there, notably the future Edward V and Arthur Tudor, both of whom did not long survive the experience. Mary Tudor, daughter of Henry VIII, also lived for a short period at Ludlow, in her capacity as heir to the throne. The choice of

Ludlow was partly due to its proximity to the border; members of the royal family were able to use its strategic position to 'govern' Wales without actually having to go there. Historically, though, the main reason for the choice was that the castle had belonged to Richard Plantagenet, duke of York, and was a family home with which his son, Edward IV, was familiar.

By the time Owain Glyndŵr came on the scene, the glory days of Edward I's castles were long in the past, but Owain seized the castle at Harlech and made it his main residence and the centre of his court for several years. He had little choice, since his own homes at Sycharth and Glyndyfrdwy had been destroyed by the English. In his last years, however, the evidence points to his having retired to Monnington Straddel in Herefordshire, where he passed away peacefully at his daughter's home. Regrettably, there are no archaeological methods capable of proving this beyond a doubt.

Owain's contemporary Henry V was born in the castle at Monmouth, but was not at that time heir to the throne. A later English king, Henry VII, was born in Pembroke Castle, once again without royal pretensions. John Leland (1506–52) wrote of having entered the bedchamber where the king was born. When, in 1485, it was time for Henry Tudor to return to Britain, he chose to land in his home county, but he never lived in Wales or spent any appreciable time there afterwards.

The Stuarts were not great lovers of Wales, and the Hanoverian kings even less so. In the nineteenth century, the royal family started coming to the principality more regularly, but there was never any thought of a home there. The British royal family did, however, renew their interest in Caernarfon Castle, and there were several royal visits. In the twentieth century, this was the venue for two investiture ceremonies, the first for the future Edward VIII in 1911, and the second for the present prince of Wales in 1969.

When Charles Windsor was invested as prince of Wales in 1969, the earl of Powis is said to have suggested Powis Castle as a future official residence for the prince. The offer was rejected, but there were good precedents. Edward VII had stayed at Powis Castle during his tenure as prince of Wales, and some window-latches in the shape of the three feathers were designed to commemorate the occasion. Edward VII's son, the future George V, also visited the castle while he was prince of Wales.

Realistically, no prince of Wales needs an official residence in Wales. Palaces are expensive to maintain, and the royal family makes a conscious effort not to be blamed for wasting public money on such fripperies. Nevertheless, a prince has to live somewhere, and there was disappointment when Prince Charles bought Highgrove in Gloucester-shire as his family home, instead of something on the Welsh side of the border. The purchase of the holiday cottage has done little to make us believe that our prince wants to spend any quality time in his principality.

# The Legacy

⤵

## PHYSICAL REMINDERS

Interaction with kings, and other members of the royal family, continues to be a prized experience despite the trend towards republicanism, as previous chapters have shown. Since Britain began its gradual merger into a United Kingdom, it has always been the case that a royal visit attracted attention and called for an official record. It is only in the past two or three centuries, however, that tangible reminders have become standard: foundation stones, statues, memorial plaques and the like. From the Victorian era onwards, the tendency has been to look back further into the past and to attempt to record events that no living person remembers. This implies a touch of dissatisfaction with our present monarchy, a feeling perhaps that the rulers of the past were more accomplished and more charismatic than our present British royal family.

The plaque in memory of the capture of Edward II at Pant-y-brad reflects its origins in a period when it was still the done thing to celebrate the activities of the English crown. It was placed before the current fashion for commemorating Wales's native royalty in art and sculpture. There are many examples of the latter: the statue of Llywelyn Fawr at Conway, the bronze of Owain Glyndŵr in the memorial garden at Pennal church, and indeed the garden itself.

The statues of Welsh heroes and heroines in the Marble Hall at City Hall, Cardiff, were unveiled in the middle of the First World War when patriotism was at its apogee, and are a striking example of an attempt to revive and give substance to a folk memory. Royal figures included in the roll of honour are Llywelyn the Last, Henry Tudor and (to many people's surprise) Boudicca, queen of the Iceni; this latter qualifies as Welsh, apparently, having been a Celt who just happened to live in the most eastern part of what is now England. Romantic and fanciful, the statues are nevertheless a work of art that attracts widespread admiration.

Likewise, the statue of King Henry V outside the Shire Hall in his birthplace is not a good likeness but is a striking piece of art. It was placed outside the eighteenth-century building in 1792. It is fitting that a town like Monmouth, which has long had difficulty deciding whether to be in

England or Wales, should be able to look back on a past when the mingling of Welsh and English blood resulted in the birth of one of Britain's most memorable kings. Without being in any way naturalistic, the statue brings Harry of Monmouth to life.

When George III celebrated his golden jubilee in 1809, it was an occasion for celebration throughout Britain. George was the first Hanoverian king to be a native Briton (an achievement in which he consciously 'gloried'). Like his father before him, he had been prince of Wales. Although neither Frederick nor his son had ever visited the principality, the incumbent prince of Wales had already, as described above, put right that omission, so there was no need for any hostility to the sitting monarch. Moreover, the only king to have lasted fifty years on the throne before George was King Henry III, who had lived during the thirteenth century, before Wales was annexed to England; the jubilee was an unprecedented event as far as the Welsh were concerned.

The people of Flintshire and Denbighshire were quick to offer their congratulations in a constructive form. They decided to erect a monument on the summit of Moel Famau, a point over 1800 feet above sea level. Lord Kenyon (1776–1855), the local bigwig, was selected to lay the foundation stone for the new monument. He was accompanied by a 500-strong contingent of the Denbighshire Volunteers, led by none other than Sir Watkin Williams-Wynn (the same grandson of the Jacobite who had welcomed the duke of Gloucester to Wynnstay a few years earlier).

The monument was designed to be seen from a long way off. One hundred and fifty feet high, and erected on the highest point of the Clwydian hills, it was to be a testament to the wealth and power of the people of that part of Wales. The Civil War was a distant echo; nothing of that kind could ever happen again. Yet the Welsh landowners still felt a need to mark out their territory. It may have been for the benefit of the French, who were once again threatening Britain's shores. This time they would find few sympathizers in Wales. It may also have been a sign to the English, just across the border, that the Welsh could do anything the rest of the kingdom could do, and do it bigger and better.

The designer was Thomas Harrison of Chester (1744–1829), who had an established reputation as an architect of public buildings, including the Lyceum Club in Liverpool and the Portico Library in Manchester. His selection for the task of designing the Jubilee Tower owed much to the work he had already done for Lord Kenyon on his grand new house on the Gredington estate. Quite what made Harrison think that an Egyptian-style monument was suitable for the purpose is hard to imagine. We must wonder whether a Welsh architect would have come up with something radically different. The unsuitability of the construction soon became apparent. In 1862, the monument's central obelisk was so badly damaged in a storm that its remains had to be dismantled. (Some would say this was a blessing.) The remaining ruined base can still be seen for miles around.

As a symbol of loyalty to George III, it was meaningless. Apart from being a block of stone, of little aesthetic merit, with no obvious symbolic connection to the monarchy, it was too far away for him to see; and photography had not yet been invented. There was no prospect of a personal visit; the elderly king was at the mercy of his deteriorating mental condition. Within two years of his jubilee, he had given up his role in government, such as it was, to his son. It was in fact the prince of Wales who had made the biggest individual donation to the cost of the monument, the sum of £105. Lord Kenyon and Sir Thomas Mostyn (1776–1831) were the next biggest contributors, with donations of £52 10s. each. Evidently the heir to the throne was determined to give twice as much as anyone else; or perhaps it was simply 'not done' to try to equal royalty.

As prince of Wales, the future George IV was one of the most prodigal in history. His grandfather, Frederick, had been generous to the point of extravagance, and had constantly quarrelled with his own parents about money. The prince regent, however, was an object lesson in how to spend without any thought as to where the next penny was coming from. In 1807, when the last member of the Stuart royal line was laid to rest at St Peter's Basilica in Rome, it was the prince of Wales who made one of the largest donations towards the erection of a marble memorial designed by the great Antonio Canova.

The prince's reputation for generosity went back even further. In 1714, the year of George I's accession to the British throne, the Society of Ancient Britons had been founded in London. Through the efforts of this society, a Welsh Charity School was set up in Clerkenwell, initially to educate twelve boys. The school later moved to Gray's Inn Road. When the future George IV, a week old, became prince of Wales in 1762, he simultaneously became a symbol of the work of the charity school. By the time he died in 1830, he had been a benefactor of the school, to the tune of 100 guineas per annum, for sixty-five years.

One of the school's most tireless workers was Richard Morris, who in 1776 actually moved into the school premises, for the benefit of his failing health. He had worn himself out in the service of the London Welsh community, putting his compatriots' welfare before that of his own immediate family. When he died three years later, he left the school all his books and manuscripts (which eventually found their way into the British Library). Another benefactor of the school was Thomas Pennant, to whom we owe much of our knowledge of Wales in the eighteenth century. Pennant's *Tours* contain all manner of information that he soaked up on his travels, including his drawings and descriptions of landmarks no longer to be seen, and his acquaintance with the local people, whom he did not consider too lowly to feature in his narrative.

For some, it was a good time to be Welsh, and the prince of Wales never scorned his principality. When, as King George IV, he visited Holyhead in 1821, the occasion was deemed so important that a public memorial was thought to be appropriate. Accordingly, a marble arch was erected at the end of the pier, marking the spot where the prince had alighted on Welsh soil. The arch, now known as Admiralty Arch, was in a similar style to, though smaller than, London's Marble Arch, and was designed by none other than Thomas Harrison. A gesture of this kind had come to be almost expected, in the reign of a man who had run up personal debts of £660,000 before he turned 35.

Nevertheless, Dr Steven Parissien, writing on the BBC website, describes George as 'a strikingly modern monarch ... in the way in which he intrinsically recognised how an attractive, manufactured image could be used to hide or divert attention from the less impressive aspects of the life of a key public figure'. It may be argued that his set, including those Welsh landowners who contributed to the erection of the hideous monument on the summit of Moel Famau, gave the same attention to their public image.

The reign of Queen Victoria ushered in many changes, but the popularity of commemorative monuments did not abate. In 1864, Tenby curried favour with the monarch by erecting a memorial to Prince Albert, who had died in 1861. The prince consort had, after all, actually visited the town. On 2 August 1865, Prince Arthur, duke of Connaught, 15-year-old son of Victoria and Albert, arrived in Tenby to dedicate the monument, which was sculpted from Welsh marble by John Evan Thomas. It was not merely Tenby's memorial to the prince consort, it was the 'Welsh national memorial', conceived by the town's mayor to ensure that Wales lived up to the example already set by the other three home countries.

In 1887, Victoria celebrated her golden jubilee. The people of Conway commemorated the event by erecting a drinking fountain alongside a bust of the queen, covered by an ornate 'canopy', a typical piece of Victoriana. In the town of Usk, the residents went one better, raising enough money by public subscription to erect a clock tower in the square, with a relief portrait of the queen on one side, to mark the occasion. The town of Monmouth waited ten years, until Victoria's diamond jubilee, to emulate Conway's example with a more classical design – minus the queen's head.

Meanwhile, in Llangollen, the parish church of St Collen installed a stained-glass window in the north aisle to mark the occasion. The parishioners no doubt felt it incumbent on them to make a physical gesture to commemorate the achievements of a queen who had taken the trouble to visit them not once, but twice, during her reign; the results can still be seen.

Standing on the seafront at Aberystwyth, outside the old University of Wales buildings, is a truly unique monument: the only known full-length statue of the prince of Wales who went on to become King Edward VIII. The statue of the sympathetic king who went down in history as saying that 'Something must be done' for the unemployed of south Wales (and promptly abdicating) has been seen by generations of students as a symbol of authority, perhaps also of Englishness, and has been the subject of several protests. The most violent of these was in 1976, shortly before Prince Charles was due to be installed as chancellor of the University of Wales, a somewhat controversial appointment. On that occasion the statue's head was removed. Having been retrieved from the ruins of Aberystwyth Castle, it had to be reattached in time for the installation of the new chancellor.

Memorials to Welsh royals are not confined within the borders of Wales. The Gwenllian memorial stone, in Sempringham, Lincolnshire, attracts visitors from the UK and overseas, evoking widespread sympathy for the princess who was confined to a convent from her earliest years, and there are proposals for an additional memorial to Gwenllian's cousin Gwladus, who lived and died at the Six Hills convent, not far away in the same county.

The most notable of these modern tributes to the royalty of Wales's past is the memorial garden at Pennal near Machynlleth, a village closely associated with Owain Glyndŵr. Glyndŵr is not the only Welsh prince commemorated there. Among others, the garden contains plaques to Owain Lawgoch, the great-great-grandson of Llywelyn Fawr who made an unsuccessful invasion attempt from France thirty years before Owain Glyndŵr proclaimed himself prince of Wales. The emphasis here is on rebellion rather than royalness.

Memorials to royal personages do not have to have the approval of the royal family. The most notable non-establishment royal of recent years was undoubtedly Diana, princess of Wales. After her divorce, and even after her death, she was still regarded as unquestioned princess of Wales. The attention she had given to Wales during her tenure of the title ensured that her memory continued to be revered within the principality even after less savoury facts about her life became public knowledge. Following the demolition of the old Cardiff Arms Park to make way for the Millennium Stadium, a shop in Gorseinon proudly displayed in its window a relic of the old stadium that it had acquired at auction: the seat in which Diana had sat when she attended international rugby matches at the Arms Park. A bust of the princess is still to be found in the foyer of St David's Hall, Cardiff, where it attracts at least as much admiration as that of her former husband.

Memorials can be less tangible things than lumps of stone. Many street names in Wales, as in the rest of Britain, bear witness to past links with the British royal family. Just as Edinburgh has Princes Street (renamed by King George III in honour of his two eldest sons), so Llandeilo has King Street, George Street and George Hill, all named after George IV in honour of his visit to the town. Cardiff's King Edward VII Avenue commemorates a visit to the capital by that king; the Alexandra Dock commemorates his queen, who opened it in 1907. Port Talbot's Princess Margaret Way and Wrexham's Prince Charles Road were named in honour of similar events.

Hotels and public houses have also been named or renamed after members of the royal family. The George IV hotel at Criccieth was built in 1830, the year the prince of Wales became king. There are of course several hundred pubs throughout Britain named 'Prince of Wales', many of them in recognition of the fact that King Edward VII was a great friend of the licensing trade. 'Queen Victoria' is also a popular name for hotels and pubs in Wales, just as it is in England; many of these were renamed at the time of Victoria's accession, jubilee or death.

In the twenty-first century, the fashion for naming licensed premises after members of the royal family has died out. The royals no longer consider it a compliment to have pubs named after them, but they do not mind having hospitals named after them. The prince and princess of Wales, not to mention Prince Philip, have all given their names to Welsh hospitals in recent years, in some cases resulting in great confusion. Port Talbot has its Princess Royal Theatre, opened by the present incumbent of that title in the 1980s. In 2002, the Queen toured south Wales during her own golden jubilee celebrations, and left Margam Park with a different kind of souvenir: a fuchsia named in her honour.

Patronage is a slightly different matter. The Royal St David's Golf Club at Harlech, founded in 1894, obtained its 'royal' status from King Edward VII. The club boasts that in 1934, while King George V was its patron, his son, the prince of Wales, was club captain! Wales's sporting connections with the royal family go back even further. In 1847, Queen Adelaide, widow of King William IV (himself nicknamed 'Sailor Bill'), gave the Royal Welsh

Yacht Club her patronage. Edward VII, a keen sailor, followed his great-aunt's example, becoming patron of the club at the age of 18 and continuing to take an interest in it when he came to the throne. His son, another famous royal sailor, George V, did likewise.

Today's royal patronage is strictly limited to official bodies and charities. The royal family tries not to be seen to be associated with any cause that it is any way questionable, and certainly not with any commercial organization. Royal regimental honours are bestowed throughout the United Kingdom, thus the Royal Regiment of Wales (which was merged with other regiments in 2006 to form the 'Royal Welsh') had no special status within the armed forces. The regiment was formed in 1969, with the prince of Wales, then aged only 20, as its colonel-in-chief. It replaced the Royal Welch Fusiliers, founded in 1689 and particularly famous for the large proportion of poets and writers it produced during the First World War.

Confusion begins to creep in when we learn that the prince of Wales also had his 'own' Regiment of Yorkshire (from the age of 10). As for the Princess of Wales's Royal Regiment, this has as its colonel-in-chief none other than the queen of Denmark! The connections with Wales are, it is clear, barely circumstantial.

A living, and more informal, reminder of Wales in the everyday life of the royal family is the Welsh corgi, a distant relative of the dachshund. The Queen was given a corgi in 1936 by her father, King George VI; she named it Dookie. Today she keeps around ten of the dogs as household pets; it has been said that she prefers them to her children. She soon began breeding them, favouring them over other breeds for their temperament. The Cardiganshire variety is supposedly on the decline, but the Queen's dogs, mostly Pembrokeshire corgis, have appeared on stamps and won awards. Jokes about the corgis abound. The Queen and her father did not choose the corgi simply because it is a Welsh breed. Nevertheless, as in the case of the Welsh gold in royal wedding rings, it did not do any harm to reinforce links with the principality, and it is doubtful whether the royal family will ever dare do away with this fairly recent tradition of corgi ownership. To stop keeping corgis would be taken as an insult to Wales.

## ARMS AND EMBLEMS

All members of the royal family, including the prince of Wales, have their own arms, devised for them by the College of Arms, a body that has been in existence since the fifteenth century. Each prince of Wales since 1301 has had his own individual arms; but the prince of Wales's feathers, as is well attested, have nothing to do with Wales. Likewise, the words 'Ich Dien', contrary to many people's belief, are not a Welsh motto. The distinctive emblem used by princes of Wales since the fourteenth century seems to have come into use as a personal symbol of the Black Prince, drawing attention to his military successes. 'Ich Dien' is a German phrase, meaning 'I serve'.

There is no record of the feathers having been used by the English royal family before the reign of Edward III, and the great Welsh herald Francis Jones believed that they first came into the Plantagenet dynasty through Edward's marriage to Philippa of Hainault. A more popular theory is that the Black Prince borrowed the emblem and its accompanying motto from King John of Bohemia, who was killed at the Battle of Crécy (the same battle in which the prince of Wales famously 'won his spurs').

There is, however, a more potent emblem of Wales that the royal family has used or adapted for use in various forms, in the form of the red dragon that appears on our flag. Dragons were popular motifs in the art of both the Romans and the prehistoric Celtic tribes. The red dragon is believed to have been used by Cadwaladr Fendigaid ('the Blessed'), a prince of seventh-century Gwynedd, and was picked up by Henry Tudor for reasons both political and sentimental, since the Tudors claimed descent from Cadwaladr, as did the House of York. King Arthur was another of those popularly believed to have used it as an emblem. As a symbol, the dragon was associated with war, and Henry Tudor's use of it signified his success as a conqueror as much as his royal birth.

The dragon featured on the royal arms of Queen Elizabeth I, but died with her. It was not until 1959 that the Queen finally recognized the red dragon on a green and white background as the official flag of the principality of Wales. Even this concession followed some heraldic disagreement and an unsuccessful attempt to introduce an alternative version which had the grudging approval of the College of Arms.

In 1896, the great patriot Owen M. Edwards bemoaned the lack of distinctive banners and bunting to decorate Welsh streets when the prince and princess of Wales came to visit. 'The lions of Llywelyn, Owen Glendower's golden dragon on a green ground ... would not these be welcome additions ...?' he asked.

More recently, a Welsh-based fashion label, named 'Red Dragonhood' by its proprietor, has sought to ring the changes. The designer expressed his view that the presence of the three-feathered badge of the prince of Wales on Welsh rugby shirts was an insult, and produced his own alternative version. The Welsh shirt, he says, should show the dragon, which he presumably regards as the true symbol of Wales.

Any search for a universally acceptable emblem for Wales is doomed to failure, as those who recall the arguments at school every St David's Day, as to whether daffodils or leeks were best, will realize. The royal standard, the arms and badge of the prince of Wales are no more than advertising logos, and have little bearing on the continued discussion of the place of the monarchy in the future of Wales.

When we look at our national flag, the images that spring to mind are not of princes or kings, but essentially relate to national identity. The dragon, for many people, symbolizes the indomitable spirit of Wales. It has no religious connotation and no particular royal connection. It is a flag that can hope to be in use for many centuries to come, regardless of whether Britain remains a monarchy and regardless of whether Wales remains part of the United Kingdom.

## INVESTITURE

We have already seen how, in previous centuries, the investitures of princes of Wales invariably took place in England, sometimes with great ceremony and celebration, and occasionally with a Welsh flavour. Yet somehow, after the fifteenth century, the direct link between the concepts of 'prince' and 'Wales' was lost, and was not fully restored until the twentieth century. All the evidence suggests that, although princes of Wales were trained as future kings, they ceased to be princes of Wales in any practical sense when they ceased to be sent to Ludlow as novice administrators.

Although it may seem that it was the twentieth century that made a media circus out of the prince of Wales's investiture, these ceremonies were the norm in the Middle Ages, and the newly created prince would often be shown to the public afterwards. It was, after all, the king's way of manifesting both his own virility and the durability of the ruling family's hold on the kingdom. The people were being allowed a chance to look at their future king, and they demonstrated their approval loudly, if contemporary accounts of the investitures are to be believed.

Edward of Middleham, the young son of King Richard III, was one of those forced to endure the onslaught of public adulation. After his investiture in York Minster, the king and queen walked hand in hand through the city streets with their little boy, dressed in all his finery. The people duly responded with 'great honour, joy and congratulations'. The next prince of Wales, Arthur Tudor, was sent on a ceremonial barge-ride down the Thames, and received similar plaudits.

By the time the Hanoverians arrived in Britain, circumstances had changed. The investiture ceremony was no more than a formality, sometimes held privately or not at all. Being prince of Wales was seldom regarded as an honour, or even as a duty, merely as one of many chores that went with the business of being heir to the throne, more welcome than most only because it carried with it a guaranteed income. When even the revenues of the principality ceased to be automatically paid, there was nothing to revel in but an empty title.

Things changed fairly suddenly with the reign of King Edward VII, who had been prince of Wales for so long that the title had come to have some meaning for him. In 1911, shortly after his death, Lloyd George persuaded the new king, George V, that not only should an investiture ceremony be held for the latest in the long line of princes, but it should be held in the principality. Called David by his family, the new prince would grow up to be king for the briefest of periods.

Francis Jones describes the 1911 investiture as 'a triumph', adding that 'Those with a feeling for history could reflect on the genealogical combin-ations and the constitutional vicissitudes that had resulted in the appearance at this ancient town of a twentieth-century prince whose ancestors, Gwyneddan and Plantagenet ... had held court on this very spot.' There was no hesitation, therefore, in arranging a similar ceremony fifty-eight years later, when David's great-nephew was invested with his title.

The security issues that surrounded the 1969 investiture were not unprecedented. Kings of England, regardless of how many bodyguards they might keep, have met violent deaths. Even the popular young King Henry V came close to being assassinated at Southampton before he set out for his victorious foray into France. After an attempt on the life of Queen Victoria in 1882, a society of New York Welshmen wrote to 'con-gratulate' her on her survival!

Charles himself would be the subject of an apparently genuine assassin-ation attempt in 1994. In 1969, the worst he had to fear was scorn, as the nationalist folk singer Dafydd Iwan lambasted him in a ditty entitled 'Carlo'. Security was tight, with 3,000 additional police officers being imported into the area, but the only casualties were two incompetent would-be terrorists who blew themselves up with their own bomb at Abergele. The prince was not their target. They knew better than to make a martyr of someone who had taken the trouble to learn the language.

Although the duke of Norfolk, in his hereditary role as 'Earl Marshal', had charge of the logistical arrangements, the chief organizer of the 1969 event was the earl of Snowdon, then brother-in-law to the Queen. Born Antony Armstrong-Jones, the earl was working as a society photographer in London during the late 1950s when he first met his future wife, Princess

Margaret. He was descended from a respectable Welsh family, his father being a barrister and his grandfather the physician Robert Armstrong-Jones. Both his paternal grandparents came from the Caernarfon area.

Snowdon's aim was not merely to replay the ceremony of 1911, but to present the modern face of the monarchy to the general public. To a 1969 audience, it may have looked like a modern 'take' on an ancient ceremony. Forty years later, the prince's futuristic gold coronet (designed by committee) and the Queen's mock-medieval hat (designed by Norman Hartnell) look dated. In time, perhaps, they will be looked back on as fashion classics.

The officially stated reason for designing a new coronet was that the one previously used was still in the possession of the duke of Windsor. It seems more likely that a coronet last used in 1911 would not only have needed a bit of a facelift, but would have presented an image of royal wealth and privilege that was not in tune with public feeling. Charles needed something more striking, less conventional, a statement of his place in history. He was seen by many, at the time, as Britain's great hope for the future, a young man who would take the monarchy forward into the twenty-first century by shedding the trappings of the past and ploughing his own furrow.

As for the Queen, the role she fulfilled in the investiture ceremony was a first for a female monarch. There had been no investiture ceremony for the son of Queen Victoria, and none of the earlier queens regnant had managed to produce any surviving male children. Rather than put on a military uniform as she might have done (George V had dressed as an Admiral of the Fleet for the 1911 ceremony), Queen Elizabeth II chose to wear a coat and hat. She had nothing to prove, and it was her son's turn to step into the spotlight.

The ceremony was watched by 4,000 people within the walls of the ruined Caernarfon Castle and an estimated 200 million more around the world, courtesy of television. This was a development the medieval kings could never have anticipated. Even in 1911, Lloyd George could not have hoped that cinema screens would enable such enormous numbers of people to witness the investiture he had devised.

Following the publication of unflattering stories about Prince William of Wales in 2008, a campaign was launched to ban any future investitures. Its organizers intend that neither William nor any other member of the British royal family will ever be prince of Wales again. *Cambria* magazine reports that 'a carefully co-ordinated royal "charm offensive" in Wales aimed at grooming Prince William for the role of the next Prince of Wales, and a "softening up" of the Welsh people for an investiture even more lavish than those of 1911 and 1969 is under way'. Support for the anti-investiture campaign seems to be limited, however. Whatever William does, many Welsh people regard it as his right to be prince of Wales when and if his father becomes king. They would rather, it seems, have any prince of Wales than none at all.

Despite the apparent desirability of continuing with the concept of the principality, no one ever seems to have proposed that any other major milestones in the life of the prince of Wales (his baptism or wedding, for example) should take place west of the River Severn. Evidently, there is a perceived demarcation zone between his life as the heir to the throne and his activities as prince of Wales.

# Today and Tomorrow

∽

In June 2007, the Queen arrived in Wales to open the new term of the Welsh Assembly, but her visit was met with protests from Plaid Cymru AMs. Leanne Wood and Bethan Jenkins declined to be present at the ceremony on the grounds that the monarchy was irrelevant to modern Wales. 'There is nothing taboo or radical about being a republican in the 21st century', Ms Jenkins was quoted as saying.

A critic responded that 'the Queen, her son and her grandson rightly hold a very special place within the hearts and affections of the Welsh people. Not only that but the individual members of The Royal Family are also our guests and are entitled to be treated as such with the same basic respect, courtesy and kindness that has made the "warm Welsh welcome" renowned right around the world.' Neil Welton, leader of the Monarchy Wales campaign, went on to suggest that any other behaviour made a laughing stock of Wales.

A quick look at the Queen's itinerary for the day bears further examination; a glance at it may help us decide whether the monarchy is, as some think, an outdated concept. Her day began with arrival at Cardiff railway station. No squeezing in and out of packed train compartments for her. She is met from the train and immediately whisked off by car to the Senedd in Cardiff Bay. Roads are closed to ensure unimpeded progress, though of course the royal vehicle travels slowly to allow the crowds to get a good look at Her Majesty.

The royal entourage is greeted with a twenty-one-gun salute from HMS *Exeter* as it arrives in Cardiff Bay and the Queen, the duke of Edinburgh, the prince of Wales and the duchess of Cornwall enter the Senedd. Inside the debating chamber, the Queen makes a speech, specially written for her, to the gathered Assembly members (not including the two Plaid Cymru renegades). After the opening ceremony and a speech from the First Minister, the royals proceed upstairs to be entertained by a local youth choir and the National Youth Symphony Orchestra of Wales. Her Majesty signs a commemorative 'parchment' to mark her visit, and is presented with flowers. Afterwards she and her party proceed to the National Museum of Wales in Cardiff, where they have lunch (in a private room, rather than the cafeteria). They make a brief tour of the exhibitions and the Queen unveils a plaque to commemorate the occasion.

Security of course dictates the Queen's movements and activities to a considerable degree. Nevertheless, one cannot help feeling as one reads this crowded programme that the people whose 'hearts and affections' are so devoted to the royal family will have little opportunity to get anywhere near them. Some would say that this is as it should be. The very fact of being royal, they would say, sets the Queen and her family apart from the rest of the population. The Queen's lifestyle, they would say, is *expected* to be different from that of her subjects. Anything less than a day full of plaque-unveiling and parchment-signing would be beneath her dignity and might even lead to a loss of status in the eyes of the public. Whether the Queen actually enjoys these enforced visits to museums and concerts, all this speech-making and waving from the window of a car, is really beside the point. It is, after all, her job.

Many members of the public, without bearing any actual hostility towards the royal family or having any kind of republican sympathies, say that they would prefer a more down-to-earth type of monarchy. The example set by Diana, princess of Wales, and by others before her, showed that this more extrovert, populist approach could work. Security never seemed to be an issue for the princess of Wales when she was carrying out her official duties, because anyone who threatened her could have expected to be torn to shreds by her adoring public. No one felt any less respect for her after she had reached into the crowd and shaken hands with them; quite the opposite.

Earlier royals were not always as remote as we tend to think. Many of the comments made about the last princess of Wales are highly reminiscent of the things that were said of one of her predecessors, Alexandra of Denmark, wife of King Edward VII. Alexandra was princess of Wales for thirty-eight years, and became so closely associated with the title that, even after becoming queen herself, she was reluctant to give it up to her son's wife. Having been brought up in Denmark, and an outsider even in the context of that country's royal family with its populist tradition, she imported a fresh spirit into the British monarchy. She visited poor families, took a particular interest in medical developments and insisted on being a 'real' mother to her own children.

Alexandra's activities, like Diana's, were noted precisely because they were different from what the people were used to seeing in their royals but, even in the nineteenth century, the monarchy was behaving differently from the way it had behaved in the past. The use of technology was just one of the symptoms of the modernization of Britain's kings and queens.

In August 1889, Queen Victoria paid one of her rare visits to Wrexham. She arrived by train at Ruabon station at 4.15 pm and travelled by road to Wrexham under a row of triumphal arches specially erected for the occasion. Flags, bunting and cheering crowds lined the road. She arrived at Acton Park to be greeted by the mayor and 'local dignitaries', including the richest people in the area who had contributed to the cost of decorating the streets and consequently had the privilege of seeing the royal entourage at close quarters. The queen was received in a special enclosed section of Acton Park, where she heard a local choir perform. Ten thousand children from local Sunday schools were allegedly present to join in the National Anthem (this of course was 'God Save the Queen'; 'Hen Wlad Fy Nhadau' had not yet been adopted as Wales's unofficial anthem).

The programme for the Victorian visit sounds suspiciously similar to the one arranged for Queen Elizabeth II in Cardiff, and indeed it is standard. The Queen is expected to arrive by private transport, with a large escort, to be received in a private area, greeted by 'local dignitaries', cheered by large crowds, entertained by large groups of performers and to show her gratitude for the attention in some practical manner. In Victoria's case, it was a knighthood for the mayor of Wrexham.

The public's attitude to the royals goes in cycles, as the death of Diana, princess of Wales, clearly showed. Ten years on, thanks largely to her portrayal on celluloid, the Queen was once more the most popular member of the royal family. It had been the same for her predecessor Victoria, mocked as the 'Widow at Windsor' but adored once again as her jubilee came round. The Hanoverians had meddled in politics. As the royal family became second- and third-generation Britons, the influences of the past faded, and the monarchy turned into a figurehead, a figurehead that had to be treated with fawning respect in order to fulfil its purpose.

Our ability to hate others decreases in proportion to their power to hurt us. Therefore, as the royals' existence becomes more symbolic and their influence over the daily life of the average person dwindles almost to nothing, our conduct towards them has changed. The nature of that change still depends very much on the individual, but it is notable that those who profess the greatest contempt for the concept of royalty are often those who show the greatest respect for the royal family when they come face to face with them.

Any member of the present royal family who visits Wales can be certain of a gushing welcome. He or she will be shown every stone of every building and expected to utter complimentary words about them, forced to eat local delicacies and to pretend to enjoy them, obliged to shake hands with every member of the crowd and to accept bouquets of flowers from them. Gone are the days when it was possible for the king of England to come and have a quick look at his subjects from the battlements of his castle, wave a hand and then retreat into privacy. Nowadays the monarch's contact with his or her people has been reduced to an occasion for ceremonial, with few opportunities for spontaneity or honest discussion. At the same time, it has become more fatiguing and less rewarding for the person who sits on the throne.

## IN CONTEXT

When Edward I invested his son with the title of prince of Wales, he was doing more than stamping his authority on the principality. He was beginning a policy of appeasement and patronage of his Welsh subjects that his successors were obliged to maintain. They could not simply ignore Wales if they wanted to govern it – they had at least to pay lip service to its significance within the realm. To do otherwise was to ask for trouble. And yet the most successful of the monarchs, in terms of keeping the peace in Wales, seem to have been those who neither patronized nor deferred to the Welsh, but simply left them to get on with things.

With the dawning of the twentieth century, the number of royal visits to Wales began to rise exponentially. It is no longer something to be remarked on if a member of the royal family sets foot in the principality, particularly if there is a new building to be opened or a special occasion to be celebrated. As for the prince of Wales, Charles turns up on a regular basis, as if checking that his stronghold is still there and in good working order. Few would suggest that he lacks commitment to the country that gave him his title.

In January 2008, writing in *Cambria*, Sion T. Jobbins reflected on the possibility of a monarchy for Wales. It was not a new idea: in 1958, D. J. Davies had come up with the proposal in an article entitled 'Wales Must Have a King' (not a monarch, we may note). Davies contended that, in order to realize the concept of an independent Wales, Plaid Cymru needed to recognize the inevitability of monarchy. He suggested that Wales cultivate its own home-grown variety.

In the *Cambria* article, Jobbins commented perceptively that 'South Wales Labourism's infatuation with royalty is only one notch below the Ulster Unionist's'. No doubt his suggestions for a new Welsh monarchy, giving ordinary people something to gossip about, were intended light-heartedly, but he revealed his own beliefs when he remarked with great hindsight that the Welsh princes 'have, over the years, opened the door to our own national dignity'. He failed to mention the squabbling of the Middle Ages, which shows Wales's royal families in a rather different light.

There will always be republicans in Wales, just as there are in the rest of the United Kingdom, but it seems likely that the royalists will remain in the majority for many years to come, even if the popularity of individual members of the royal family fluctuates. The prince of Wales's sons, William and Harry, despite their tender age, have both already undergone periods of difficulty and damage to their public image. Within Wales, they are recognized as having a special status because of the title their father holds. They will do well to look back at the example set by the most successful of their ancestors and remember their Welsh blood. It will stand them in good stead when they find themselves most in need. There is always a welcome in the hillsides, for those who remember to look.

# Select Bibliography

## BOOKS

Abse, Joan (ed.), *Letters from Wales* (Seren, 2000)

Cannon, John and Griffiths, Ralph, *The Oxford Illustrated History of the British Monarchy* (Oxford University Press, 1998)

Davies, R. R., *The Age of Conquest: Wales 1063–1415* (Oxford University Press, 1987)

Davis, Paul R., *Castles of the Welsh Princes* (Y Lolfa, 2007)

Fisher, Deborah, *Princes of Wales* (University of Wales Press, 2006)

Fisher, Deborah, *Princesses of Wales* (University of Wales Press, 2005)

Jenkins, Geraint H., *A Concise History of Wales* (Cambridge University Press, 2007)

Jones, Francis, *The Princes and Principality of Wales* (University of Wales Press, 1969)

Jones, Gareth Elwyn, *Modern Wales* (Cambridge University Press, 1984)

Kightly, Charles, *A Mirror of Medieval Wales: Gerald of Wales and his Journey of 1188* (Cadw, 1988)

Maund, Kari, *The Welsh Kings: The Medieval Rulers of Wales* (Tempus, 2004)

Parissien, Steve, *King George IV: The Grand Entertainment* (John Murray, 2001)

Parry, Edward, *Royal Visits and Progresses to Wales* (Edward Parry, 1850)

Plumptre, George, *Edward VII* (Pavilion, 1995)

Soulsby, Ian, *The Towns of Medieval Wales* (Phillimore, 1983)

Turvey, Roger, *The Welsh Princes 1063–1283* (Longman, 2002)

Tytler, Sarah, *Life of Her Most Gracious Majesty the Queen* [Victoria)](repr. Bibliobazaar, 2007)

Vaughan-Thomas, Wynford, *The Princes of Wales* (Kaye & Ward, 1983)

Weir, Alison, *Britain's Royal Families: The Complete Genealogy* (Pimlico, rev. edn. 1996)


## WEBSITES

*http://www.itvlocal.com/wales* – film archive of the Queen's visits to Wales

*http://www.monarchywales.org.uk*

# Index